For Fred ~
A Fellow

Warmest regards

Christopher deVinck

*Love's Harvest*

February 20, 2011

Pompton Plains. NJ

M000031125

# Love's Harvest

## Family, Faith, Friends

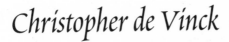

*Christopher de Vinck*

*A Crossroad Book*
The Crossroad Publishing Company
New York

The Crossroad Publishing Company
370 Lexington Avenue, New York, New York 10017

Printed in the United States of America

Library of Congress Cataloging-in-Publication Data

De Vinck, Christopher, 1951–
    Love's harvest : family, faith, friends / by Christopher de Vinck.
      p.  cm.
    ISBN 0-8245-1749-0 (pbk.)
    1. Family—Religious aspects—Catholic Church.  2. Faith.
  3. Friendship—Religious aspects—Christianity.  4. De Vinck,
Christopher, 1951–  .  5. Catholic Church—Doctrines.  I. Title.
BX2351.D39  1998
242—dc21
                                         98-9847
                                           CIP

1 2 3 4 5 6 7 8 9 10 02 01 00 99 98

# *Contents*

Introduction    1

## Family   ∿   5
Family    7
Family of Christmas    10
Family in Silence    13
Family Under the Stars    17
Easter Family    20
Family Ties    24

## Faith   ∿   29
Faith    31
Faith in Goodness    34
Faith in the Snow    37
Faith in Who We Once Were    39
Faith in the Routine    42
Faith in What Is Lost    46
Faith in Self    50
Faith in Marriage    53
Faith in God    58
Faith in the Moon    60
Faith in Prayer    63
Faith in the Turtle    69
Faith When We Are Hungry    72
The Lack of Faith    79

# Contents

**Friends ～ 83**

Teacher as Friend    85

My Friend May Sarton    92

The Friendship of a Stranger    96

The Luck of a Brother-in-law as a Friend    101

Friendship with a Stubborn Grandfather    106

The Goodwill of America    113

Husband as Best Friend    119

Ah, the Girlfriend    123

Wife as Best Friend    128

Sister as Friend    132

The Love of a Friend    138

Tokens of Friendship    142

Brother as Friend    145

The Friendship of the Father    148

The Friendship of the Mother    151

Children as Friends    155

Antigone, My Friend    172

**Conclusion ～ 177**

# Introduction

❧

When I was nine I understood for the first time that I might someday die. Because my uncle, a man I never met, had recently dropped dead from a heart attack on the streets of Paris, I suddenly had doubts about my own mortality. This notion stayed with me through the spring and summer of that year.

In the fall I decided that I had to know for sure if *I* was going to die someday, so I developed a system that would let me know. My plan was to build a small raft with sticks the size of my fingers and then to float the raft down the one foot wide stream that cut its way through the middle of the garden where I grew up. If the raft reached the waterfall, I reasoned, I would not die, but if the raft beached itself against the shore or snagged itself on the rocky bottom and didn't reach its destination, then I would know that, yes, I would indeed someday die.

After I grabbed scissors from the kitchen drawer, I ran out the back door, and down the porch stairs, and into the garden. I ran to my right, rushed beyond the pricker bushes, through the small gate, then I stood under the great maple tree that leaned over the house. I reached up for the tip of a branch. After I cut fifteen small sticks, I sat on the ground and wove the bits of maple into a miniature raft, the grand sea vessel that would predict my fate.

I had at the time a small, yellow book about myths in my room. It spoke of an ancient ritual during the mid-summer festivals in Europe where people floated down rivers in flower-covered boats. That seemed like a logical way to discover what was at the end of the river, so when I finished making my raft, I stuck a late fall rose in the middle of the raft, and then I ran to the stream.

It had been a particularly wet autumn, so the stream was full and quick as it swirled down the gentle slope toward the small waterfall and pond my father had constructed.

When I reached the source of the stream in the hill, I leaned over and brushed my hand back and forth in the water, I the wizard about to conjure up secrets that slipped through the cool wetness; then I set my raft and flower into the water. Immediately they flowed silently and with confidences from my hands, the rose bobbing up and down as the maple sticks wobbled along the top of the uneven water.

I followed the raft, urging it forward, almost daring to push the water behind with my cupped hand, but knowing that I could not interfere with fate. For a brief moment it seemed as if the raft and rose would be caught along the edge of a small curve in the stream, but then they just twirled around and around and spun into the center of the stream and continued on their way.

How often do we feel lost, unsure of our destiny, but how often do we also feel that, at least, we are moving in some direction?

Closer, closer, the raft floated toward the small waterfall. I ran ahead, stopped, kneeled down and watched my little raft and rose rush up to the very edge of the waterfall then, whoosh, down they rolled into the tumult until they arrived upright and safe in the calm pool of water. I was *never* going to die.

## Introduction

With that settled, I cupped my hand, drank some of the cool water, felt the life force rush down my throat, and then I climbed the small hill and ran home.

Today I am forty-five years old and the stream in my father's garden has been dry for ten years. Autumn is my favorite season because of the contrasts: color and darkness, heat and sudden cold. Even the moon is different in autumn, full of a light that is defined in the belly of a pumpkin or through the newly bare trees.

The harvest will sustain us through the winter. Children return to school. The air contains an ancient power that calls us all back to reconsider our common routines.

In the fall we also look toward winter with hidden dread, and yet there are still moments of great beauty as we shuffle our shoes through dried leaves scattered against the gray sidewalk as we remember the sound of rushing water and the scent of the sweet, summer rose.

This book is a collection, a harvest of love that I have gathered along the way while shuffling through the leaves of a life that is scattered before me.

I hope you hear the sound of rushing water in my words, and smell the sweet summer rose as you turn each page. I hope this little book leads you to your own harvest of family, faith, and friends.

# ~ *Family* ~

*I am part of the sun as my eye is part of me.*
*That I am part of the earth my feet know*
*perfectly, and my blood is part of the sea. My*
*soul knows that I am part of the human race,*
*my soul is an organic part of the great human*
*race, as my spirit is part of my nation. In my*
*very own self, I am part of my family.*

D. H. Lawrence

# Family

⌒

I can understand why archeologists are excited when they discover evidence of lost civilizations: hidden walls, broken pots, weapons cut from stone. They brush the dirt away and lift the past from the forgotten dust, attaching stories and explanations to hidden treasures that seem, somehow, connected to who we are as a people today.

My brothers and sisters and I were amateur explorers of ancient times when we met at my parents' house this winter to clean out the attic.

The house my parents bought in 1948 is a three-story turn-of-the-century building with a porch, wide windows, and brown cedar shingles. It is the house where six children grew, formed alliances with each other, collected rocks and stamps, endured prom photographs, celebrated birthdays, smelled the wisteria flowers during warm spring nights.

With the passing years, the scenery of our childhood, adolescent, and college days was transported to the attic, and then we all moved out to our own homes where new civilizations were created and new children began collecting their own artifacts.

"We're going to clean out Mom's attic," my sister Marie suggested on the phone, and, a few weeks later, we were up in my parent's attic with brooms and vacuum cleaners, plastic bags, empty boxes, and a few regrets.

My mother opened a metal trunk she and my father had brought over from Belgium. The New Jersey address was still stenciled in white on the side of the trunk, along with the name of the ship they used to cross the Atlantic Ocean: *Queen Elizabeth.*

"Here is the coat I wore when we arrived," my mother said as she pulled up the black piece of worn clothing from the old trunk. "It was February, in the middle of the great winter of 1948. There were icebergs floating in the Hudson River."

My father fished out his tuxedo, the one he wore as a young man in the ballrooms of Brussels. He brushed his hand along the coat, then returned it to the metal trunk.

Michael, my eleven-year-old son, said, "Hey! What's this?" He had discovered a small wind-up train engine my brother and I used as we connected miles of track around the living room and dining room when he and I were, well, eleven years old. My brother and I, after a moment's hesitation, gave the engine to Michael.

We found high school yearbooks, copies of the Hardy boys' adventures, high school pictures of boy friends and girl friends at the shore, college textbooks, research papers, posters of the Beatles, extra wedding vases, stacks of *National Geographic* magazines and *New Yorker* magazines. My sister displayed one of her first art projects, a design for the high school play, "Welcome to the Monkey House." My brother found his old tennis racquet; I found letters my mother wrote to me when I was in college, words of family news and encouragement. One letter still had a five-dollar bill tucked inside.

Archeologists have made extraordinary discoveries: Sumerian tablets, paintings from Pompeii, third-millennium-B.C. sculptures, ancient slate palettes for cosmetics, bronze daggers from the Shang Dynasty, papyrus documents, the

Rosetta Stone, terra-cotta figures of warriors and horses, pottery, weaving, statues of ivory and gold. But all these things do not mean as much to me as watching my mother say, "Oh, let's throw out that old coat," or Michael walking down the stairs with the wind-up engine in his hand, or old photographs of the girl I dated in high school being thrown out with most of the other useless items of the little tribe that grew up in New Jersey and continues to do the best we can as we all headed home to our own little fires and ancient memories dancing above us in the stars that have been watching over us all along through this tired century that is soon coming to a close.

Perhaps millions of years from now archeologists will be digging along the outer countryside along the Hudson River and will come upon wooden walls covered in cedar, and they will unearth a metal truck and find a coat and tuxedo entwined together and they might write in their notebooks, "Twentieth-century structure. Evidence of a marriage and a voyage from Europe. Possible family dwelling."

# Family of Christmas

❧

In 1948, after my parents immigrated from Belgium, they moved into their house in Allendale, New Jersey. They arranged their furniture, unrolled the carpets, and hung along the wall of the front stairs six Japanese prints, beautiful blue engravings of Japanese women in ceremonial robes, a gift from my grandfather, who had traveled around the world when he was a young man. Forty-eight years later, these framed illustrations still hang on the same wall, on the same nails, with the same wire, in the same house.

Also in 1948, I'm told, my father and mother drove to the local nursery and picked out their first American Christmas tree, a balsam pine: short needles, tall, round, fresh. The attendant tied the tree to the roof of their car, and they drove home.

Together, the Japanese pictures and the Christmas tree are locked in my memory as things that belong to Norman Rockwell, Hallmark greeting cards, *Reader's Digest,* Jimmy Stewart, and the Ford Motor Company.

My father pulled a silver bucket out from under the sink the day before Christmas in 1948, filled it with five or six large rocks, wedged the trunk of the Christmas tree between the rocks, and placed the tree and bucket in the center of the living room.

# Family

Each year my parents drove in their Ford station wagon to the nursery and bought their tree, the same tree it seemed to me. Each year my father collected the same rocks, which he kept under the front porch, and each year he placed the tree and the bucket in the exact same spot in the center of the living room. I knew it was the same spot for we could see, all year round, the circle in the carpet where the bucket sat each December.

As I grew up, the Ford wagon continued to carry my sisters and brothers and me to the nursery as we all selected a tree, just the right one . . . balsam pine, short needles, tall, round, fresh.

On Christmas morning it was the tradition in our house that we had to wait for everyone to wake before we could rush down the stairs, and each Christmas I was the first one up. I'd jump out from my covers, shake my brother in the bed across the room, and run to the top of the stairs. There I would wait for everyone else. They had to stand behind the first one in line: me.

As I waited for my brothers and sister to leap from their beds, and for my parents to be roused, I sat on the top step and did what I did each Christmas: I looked at the distorted Christmas tree in the reflection of the glass that covered the Japanese prints. I could make out the tree's outline, the bulbs, the tinsel, just like the trees I saw in the famous drawings of Norman Rockwell in the *Saturday Evening Post* that sat on the coffee table.

One year my sister Anne and I made Christmas trees out of old *Reader's Digest* magazines. We were shown in school how to fold each page, and then how to spray the finished product. That was our Christmas gift to my mother that year.

Nostalgia is the exemplar of things past, not an accurate measure of reality, but a mere taste of pleasure once lived.

This Christmas I will be at my parents house once again for the forty-fifth time. My father is in his mid-eighties; my mother is in her mid-seventies; and I, well, I am eight, and I am standing at the top of the stairs looking at the distorted Christmas tree through the looking glass. And there is Anne, my sister—yes, she is ten—holding her *Reader's Digest* tree up to my mother, and my father just drove down the driveway in his Ford wagon with Tiny Tim on his shoulders perhaps.

Am I George Bailey in Frank Capra's film *It's a Wonderful Life* groping for Zuzu's petals, calling out to Clarence, standing by the Christmas tree with my own daughter as a bell rings: "Look, Daddy. Teacher says every time a bell rings an angel gets his wings."

Am I Norman Rockwell painting a holiday scene through an open window of a boy leading his brothers and sisters down the stairs past the Japanese smiles on his way to Christmas past?

I like to remember the way things were, and I am grateful that my parents are still alive, and that they are still living in the same house. Nothing has changed, really, not even the boy.

We try hard as adults to act our age, to bury foolish ideas and dreams, but each Christmas, just as the Hallmark corporation asks us to do with their pretty cards, I check the back of my own heart to make sure that the child I was and the adult I am is still the genuine product of my mother and father, who hoped that their beliefs in what is simple and good and brave and wise have made a difference in the child they gave over to a world that easily forgets the glow of the Christmas tree after December 25.

# Family in Silence

⌒

Often when I step outside to carry the trash to the garbage can that waits with its gaping mouth along the side of the garage, I see a chipmunk zoom across the driveway and drop down into a hole just to the left of the concrete slab near the stone steps.

What does a chipmunk hear as it rolls itself into its burrow while a 170-pound human being thuds down on the ground above the creature? Surly it hears the thump of my heavy shoes as I pass inches above its sanctuary. My grandmother remembered how the earth vibrated each time a Nazi bomb dropped somewhere close to home. "The earth shook. I could feel it."

We are placed in circumstances where the solid parts of our world are disturbed by shifting priorities, mood swings, or by simple fate. All seems in hand, and then suddenly it is lost, sand passing between our fingers. What to do when the deal is lost or gained, the deal of marriage, or corporate merger, or promises made over a handshake or signature? I think the answer can be had as we sit in the silence and listen.

One morning, after I once again dumped the trash in the garbage pail, I walked above the chipmunk hole, climbed the stairs back into the kitchen. After I closed the door, I stopped, turned, and slowly parted the curtains and waited. The chipmunk waited too, perhaps anxious to see if the silence was consistent. Within five minutes, the animal popped out of its shelter, ran to a small tree stump, sat on top, and began preening its fur, scratching behind its neck, and then it ran into the grass, tail up, in search of nuts and insects again. In the silence we can define the meaning of the noise that surrounds us.

I too felt the drubbing vibration above me, a breaking of the silence. A few months ago, during a low time in my own mood swings, a time when I left my twenty-one-year career in education to pursue my writing, I went to bed early simply because I was tired of the deal I made with myself, and fearful that, perhaps, I had made a mistake. That was a Friday night.

The next morning I woke up to a distant hum of an engine. I turned to my wife, Roe, and said, "What is a helicopter doing so early in the morning?" The sound was off a great distance, a quick, steady thrumming, a low growl of power and motion. I tried to go back to sleep, but the engine's noise was too consistent, and it was increasing in volume.

"It's worse than the garbage trucks waking us up," I complained as I pushed back the window shade. "Hey, it sounds as if it is coming right over the house. Why would a helicopter fly so slowly over the house?" Suddenly I could feel a slight vibration in the room, then I looked up through the tall oak trees that formed a canopy of leaves above the yard. The engine throbbed wonderfully. I looked and looked up through the trees and tried to make out the object creeping over the house. "Roe? That's *not* a helicopter."

Did you ever see something you could not, at first, name, could not exactly identify? This shape, this thing, each time I looked closer it grew bigger and bigger until I yelled, "It's a blimp! Hey, it's the Goodyear blimp! Roe, it's flying right over the house! Look how low it is! This is great!" The silver skin, the large letters GOODYEAR, the gondola. It was just like a scene from a movie.

# Family

"I bet if I could, I'd be able to climb the trees and pull myself right into the cabin. Look at that, Roe." It passed over the house like a slow, great whale. Then I thought, Michael.

I jumped out of bed in my checkered pajamas and ran toward the room of my eleven-year-old son. I pushed his door open and cried out, "Michael!"

Well, the boy was sleeping. He was visibly shaken when he awoke. "Dad, you scared me."

"Come outside with me. A blimp. Come see the blimp."

Michael leaped out of bed and looked through his window."

"No, come on. We'll be able to see it better out in the road in the front of the house!"

Michael and I ran down the stairs, opened the front door, and stood in the middle of the street. "Look at that, Michael. Look at the size of that machine!" Michael was equally impressed. We felt the vibrations from the engine piece into us. I thought the ground shook. It felt wonderful.

As the blimp slowly made its way into the distance, Michael took my hand and said, "Dad, you're in your pajamas." I looked down at my bare feet and laughed.

When Michael was six, he would often knock on his wall in the morning while I shaved in the bathroom. His room was just behind the bathroom mirror. If Michael knocked three times, I would knock three times in response. The sound that passed through the wall was all that a father could hope for in a lifetime.

After the war, my grandmother said that she liked to listen to the silence. "All the church bells in Brussels rang when the war was over, and then things slowly returned to normal, and there were times, again, to sit in the silence."

Now whenever I shave, the wall is silent. Michael has forgotten our secret code. I have lived in this house for twenty years, and the GOODYEAR blimp passed overhead just once. My grandmother is dead, buried in the soil of Belgium that was pounded again and again with the vibrations of bombs and explosions. Now all is silent.

Each day we make deals, sign contracts, hope something will succeed, work hard at making a sale, try to predict the value of a commodity, offer services, but what do we think on our return home?

Chipmunks sit and wait for the security of silence. I think of the man who looks in the mirror as he shaves and remembers the sound of his boy knocking on the wall three times.

I think of the man who stands in the middle of the street in his pajamas and bare feet, and then I say that yes, life is indeed a deal, a contract, a bargain, a commodity to evaluate each day, and it is best, it seems to me, to make a final judgment in the silence. For it is in the silence that we can decide if we have been a rogue or a person who believes that bells and blimps, grandmothers, chipmunks and children contain the true dividends of success. It is all discovered in the vibrations we feel as we sit in silence in the late afternoon on our way home.

# Family Under the Stars

ᝨ

I have been missing the significance of ordinary events lately, preoccupied with a comet and the pope.

It has been reported in *The New York Times* that if I look out my door in the northeastern sky, I will be able to see Comet Hale-Bopp, which is traveling at 186,282.4 miles per second. I was impressed. It has been estimated that this comet is twenty-five miles in diameter and will not return to the relative vicinity of earth for about three thousand years.

I have been keeping track of the comet in the newspapers, looking at the charts, illustrations, and photographs of the burning mass of materials and gas. The evening television news programs have given the comet a prominent place in their story lineup. There is even a place to find information on this comet's movement on the Internet. I have been sucked up into the comet's influence, not a gravitational pull, or a scientific magnetism, just a little sense of self-importance: the comet needs my attention in order for it to accrue significance.

While I was fiddling with the computer, trying to set up the machine for my daily visit to the Internet's tracking of the comet, I scrolled through a few files and came upon a piece my daughter, Karen, wrote for her eighth-grade English teacher. It was a small, biographical piece, and among the wonderful lines defining her sense of inner strength, her hopes for the future, and a description of her friends, she slipped in a line, "And I'm going to have my room painted: silk purple." Silk purple? I promised her over four months earlier that I would paint her room silk purple.

The comet Hale-Bopp is at least four times bigger than Halley's Comet.

The next morning, after I took my shower, I stepped up to my wife's mirror and dresser, searching for the red comb that we have shared for nearly twenty years. I found a thin, ordinary blue comb where the red comb always sat, and after a few seconds, I found the old comb in the trash basket. I picked it up out of the garbage and saw that two of the middle tines in the comb were broken. I tossed the comb back into the basket and thought about the pope.

A few days before, I had been invited to speak in the Vatican at the Pontifical Council for the Family. Then I received further word that I was asked if I would personally give my book *The Power of the Powerless* to Pope John Paul II in a private meeting. As I dressed, I was thinking about what I would wear to the Vatican.

I discovered that it is easy for me to fall into a pattern of self-congratulation, while ignoring what is happening around me. For the past weeks my eleven-year-old son, Michael, has been spending his time and interest on the re-released Star Wars movies. He bought some of the Star Wars action figurines, I've taken him to the movies, he's been reading some of the Star Wars adventure books. Last week Michael asked about the Star Wars poster we hung long ago in the basement television room, along with posters of *The Wizard of Oz, The Secret Garden,* and *Gone with the Wind.* I know he didn't come right out and say that he wished that he could have that poster in his room.

Who else will be invited to the Vatican, I thought. I wonder if I'll have a bit of time to visit Rome? Perhaps I'll swing north and visit relatives in Belgium.

Last night, as I leaned over Michael and turned off his light, he said something about the Star Wars poster again. I look at him though the darkness in his room, through my own glowing thoughts of the pope and the comet, then, suddenly, something got through, a small voice: "I love you, Daddy."

I leaned over Michael and kissed his cheek. I went into Karen's room and kissed her good night, walked past David's room (seventeen-year-old-don't-even-shake-my-hand) and said, "Good night, David." From deep within the mystery of calculus homework and Pink Floyd I heard a distinct, "Good night." Each week during the Easter season, I bought David a cream-filled Cadbury chocolate egg.

"Did you know," I said to Roe as I crawled into bed next to her, "that it takes eleven minutes for the light from that comet to reach earth?"

"Good night, Chris," she said as I gave her a long back rub.

The next day I bought a new comb and placed it on Roe's dresser, and a chocolate egg and placed it on David's pillow. I painted Karen's room silk purple and carried a Star Wars poster up from the basement and tacked it on the smooth surface of Michael's bedroom wall.

There is no terrestrial light more illuminating than a smile from my wife and children as they make their way through the universe of themselves under the gaze of a caring father and a loving husband who is reminded to look inward for true claims of victory, not out toward the stars.

# Easter Family

∾

When I was a teacher I could not reconcile my wish to help my students become reflective people with the knowledge that the more reflective we become the more open we are to sadness.

A contemplative life invites the shadows into our inner world, the world of the soul that is open to both what is good and to what is dark and destructive. We do build up armor against such ruinous forces by the accumulation of wisdom, but such wisdom comes with a price: the realization that perfection does not exist, that we have to make compromises, that we see more and more what could be and have to accept the reality of what is, for it is in such acceptance that we come to tie together who we are and who we wish to be, what we want and what we have, where we are and where we wish we could be.

As I look out my window I see the wind shaking the leaves. A crow, flying against the wind, hovers in mid-air over my neighbor's house, leaves roll down the street like children doing cartwheels. The force of winter recedes to the force of spring, fighting out the battle in my front yard. This resembles my own struggles as I too try to manage the divergent seasons of myself.

I want to be a child still, and yet the world wants me to be an adult. I've done fairly well, marrying a woman who loves and tolerates me. We are raising three good children who please us daily, I am juggling a career in education with a career in writing, but I also still want to be a child. I want to run outside in the wind with my sister Anne and pretend that we are caught in a hurricane as we did when she was ten and I was eight. I want to see how many goose eggs we can find in the swamp and mark the nest's location in my mind so that I can return in a few weeks and see the goslings.

Between winter and spring there is a sense that we are giving up something: the harsh cold to the smell of warm earth, the stark beauty of snow to the mud and rain. We need a season between the seasons, taking what is best, let's say, from winter and combining that with what is best from spring. How nice to pick daffodils in a snow-covered field. How good to ice-skate in seventy degree weather.

This past Easter I was reminded how far I've come from the days when I ran to a clump of grass hoping to find a chocolate egg wrapped in silver as my father pointed with his finger to the spot just to the right.

My mother is seventy-five years old. My father is eighty-five years old. On Easter my brother Bruno and my sister-in-law Lori and their son Marc and his fiancee, Christa, stood around the dining-room table along with my sister Anne and my brother-in-law John and their sons Matthew, Dan, and Michael, along with my other sister, Maria, and my brother-in-law Peter and their children Christopher and Sarah, my brother Jose, and my son David and my daughter Karen. We all stood around the Easter table as our friend, Fr. John Catoir, thanked God for the food, for the family, for the time together. My wife, Roe, was home with Michael. They both had strep, and they both insisted that David, Karen, and I ought not to miss Easter.

This was one of the few times that I was at a family function without Roe. She was out there somewhere. I was home with my brothers and sisters. When I arrived at the front door and hugged my sister Anne, I felt like asking, "Wanna go look for goose eggs?"

During the day my brother Bruno spoke with great enthusi-
asm about his growing autograph collection. I felt like asking
him, "Wanna go see our names that you scratched in the
kitchen window thirty years ago?"

When my brother Jose spoke about completing his extraordinary book about exchange theory, I felt like asking him if he
wanted to just go outside and pick some daffodils.

During the traditional Easter egg hunt, I watched my
youngest niece, three-year-old Sarah, stoop and pick up
chocolate eggs that my father had hidden in the grass. I was
hoping that he would look at *me* and point to a certain clump
of grass, but he didn't.

For a moment I stepped away from the others as they made
their way through the garden. I sat on a small rock wall my
father built fifty years ago. I looked at my family, my brothers
and sisters, their husbands and wives, the various children in
various stages, eating candy, laughing, talking. Then I realized
that I am no different than I was when I was Sarah's age. I am
still a three-year-old boy hunting in the grass for the bits of
delicious chocolate my father hid. I am still seventeen years
old, throwing jelly beans at my sister's head as she makes her
way past the apple tree. I am a forty-five-year-old man sitting
on a wall as my thirteen-year-old daughter steps up and says,
"Come on, lazy bones."

I looked at this young woman standing before me and I felt
that wind rushing around me, that wind that keeps the crow
up in mid-air, that wind that pushes the leaves. I felt my
daughter's hand as she pulled me up from the wall, and I felt
the best that spring has to offer: hope, warmth, the hair of a
young girl bouncing on her shoulders as she stoops down,
picks up a chocolate egg, and hands it to her father. "Happy
Easter, Daddy," Karen whispers, and suddenly I don't care that
I am not three or seventeen. I am content, filled with a deep
sense of contemplation as I look at this girl, this woman, this

daughter I call mine, but she is not mine. She belongs to spring and to the future and to all that waits for her.

I looked at my eighty-five-year-old father and thought, "What must he think as he sits on the wall and considers the day?"

After the Easter egg hunt I called Roe to see how she was doing. I woke her up.

"That's okay. I had to get up anyway. I was reading on the couch and I just fell asleep. Michael and I are fine. Are you having a good time?"

It was impossible to speak over the phone about the twenty years we have so far spent together. It was impossible to speak about the chocolate eggs. It was impossible to explain to Roe that I saw a glimpse of paradise, but I did say this in response to her question: "Yes, I am having a very nice time, and I am so glad to hear your voice. I'll be home soon."

"Don't rush. Stay as long as you like. Michael and I are going to have a bit of dinner. We're not very hungry. Then we're going to watch some television."

"Okay. I love you."

"I love you too. See you in a while."

I hung up the phone and walked into the living room of my youth, sat on the couch between my brother and sister. My father adjusted his hearing aid. My mother passed around some recent photographs. I ate a chocolate egg and felt just fine, not sad, not happy, just content, reflective, a bit cautious, older, with my soul intact, held together with the hand of my daughter, the voices of my wife and sons, the images of my brothers and sisters, the memory of my father as a young man stooping over next to me in the garden as he whispers, "There's a marshmallow rabbit under that piles of leaves."

What a garden it was; what a garden it is, the garden of Eden, the garden of paradise, the garden of my youth, the garden of memory. What we take out from such a place and what we add determines the condition of our soul. I think my soul is made of chocolate.

# Family Ties

࠾

Every Friday afternoon my parents shopped for the weekly food supply. "Behave, and don't let anyone in the house," my mother instructed as she dropped her shopping list into her purse and snapped it shut.

One afternoon, as the station wagon pulled out of the driveway, my sister Anne asked, "Want to play Monopoly?"

"Nah," I said as I dove onto the living-room couch.

"How about Hearts?"

"Nah."

"You wanna make a castle with the couch pillows?"

"Anne, leave me alone. I'm not interested in any baby games."

"You're never interested in anything. You're such a lazy bum." My sister grabbed a pillow and threw it at my head.

I picked up the pillow, replaced it in its proper place on the couch, looked at Anne, smiled and walked up to my room. I fell backward onto my bed and looked up at the hanging World War II bomber I had made the year before from a plastic model-building kit my grandfather had bought for me on my birthday. I'll take care of his army, I thought as I stood on the bed, reached up, grabbed the tail of the airplane and yanked it from its plastic cord, which was attached to a ceiling hook.

## Family

The plane was called the Flying Fortress, which never made sense to me. How could a fort fly? My brothers and sisters and I had tree forts, grass forts, box forts. We never thought about adding wings to any of our forts.

My model-building experiences were limited to the construction of a plastic robin and the World War II bomber. The robin was easy to build. There were two main pieces which, when snapped together, formed the entire body of the bird. The legs had to be glued, and the wings had to be snapped into place. What I liked best about the robin was the painting, but even that was easy for all I had to do was follow a color chart that indicated exactly where the brown, gray, and yellow paint ought to be applied. I suppose life would be much easier if it came with little numbers and painting instructions.

The bomber was more difficult to paint than the robin, especially the windows. I would like to know anyone who ever built a model who didn't smear the plastic windows with glue.

I was bored and tired of looking at that plane hanging from my ceiling. What if I pretended the plane had a terrible accident in the sky, I thought, with my grandfather at the controls.

I stepped out of my room, with the bomber under my arm, and walked down the narrow hallway toward my parents' bedroom. Beyond their room, through the French doors, a terrace jutted out under the maple tree branches. I opened the outer door and walked onto the balcony.

I leaned over the white railing and looked down from my second-story perch. At first I thought I'd just toss my airplane over the side and watch it smash down on the stones, but then I had an even better idea.

I placed the bomber on the floor of the balcony, and then I ran into the house. After I raced down the front stairs, I quickly ran into the kitchen pantry. I found what I was looking for: matches. They were carefully stored in a plastic box behind the salt.

I grabbed a single book of matches and ran back upstairs to the balcony.

"Chrissy!" Anne called from the living room. I ignored her. I was on an important mission: the destruction of the Belgian Air Force over the tall Alps..

I lifted the plane by its tail, then tucked it under my arm as I tried to strike a paper match, which I finally managed to do. I held the match in my right hand and held the airplane in my left hand. I thought it would be best if I lit the right wing of the plane, and then I would heave it over the rail and watch it spiral and twist in flames down, down, down to its final doom against the rocks of my grandfather's garden.

As I held the wing in the yellow flame, I began to have my doubts. Would the plane burn after all? But then, magically, thick, black smoke began to curl up the side of the aircraft. I blew out the match and threw it over the side. I held the bomber above the edge and was about to toss that down too when I heard a small sound: *ziiiip*. I looked over the edge and saw a small ball of fire drip from the wing tip and drop down two stories into the leaves below. The wing was now melting. A tall plume of black smoke rose above me. I didn't realize that plastic burned and melted at the same time. Molten plastic curled off the burning airplane and dripped to the ground accompanied by a *zip, zip, zip* sound.

"Hey, what are you doing?"

I turned and there was Anne standing in the doorway about to ruin the most spectacular episode in aviation history.

"Go away."

"Make me." She stepped onto the balcony. "Boy, are you gonna get it!"

By now the entire right wing of the airplane was in flames and many more globs of plastic were *zip, zip, zipping* down on their final descent. Sarah leaned over the edge. "Chrissy! The leaves are burning!"

I, too, leaned over and was startled to see that the leaves
were indeed burning, and the flames were spreading in all
directions, particularly in the direction of the house. I didn't
want to appear frightened and weak, so I just said, "Big deal."

"You're going to burn the house down!"

I gave Anne a calm, movie-star look, smothered the flame
of the burning airplane, and tossed it over. It landed in the rose
trellis.

"Anne, you're such a baby. Big deal. A little fire." I stole
one more look over the rail. The flames began to lick the
bottom clapboards of the house. I stuck my hands in my
pockets, turned, and slowly walked off the balcony, but not
until I turned to Anne and repeated, "No big deal."

The moment I stepped into the house, I ran through my
parents' bedroom, and nearly dove down the front stairs. My
heart pumped faster and faster. I was about to burn down the
house!

I ran outside. Fortunately, the garden hose was already
attached to the outside spigot. I spun the faucet handle like a
madman and ran with the squirting hose, which shot water out
before me in a steady stream. I ran through the gate, past the
back porch, turned the corner, and was about to run down the
garden steps to the fire, when the hose ceased its cooperation
and I was tugged to the ground. The hose was too short.

I stood up and saw, beyond the rose trellis, tall, yellow
flames that outlined the southern foundation of the house. I
picked up the hose and aimed the shooting water into a high
arch that barely reached the flames.

When the final bit of fire had been extinguished, I dropped
the hose, leaped over the stone wall, and ran to the smolder-
ing leaves.

There was a two-foot black path of burned leaves at the
base of the house. I dropped to my hands and knees and
began to brush the ashes into the dirt. I then reached over and

grabbed unburned leaves and began to scatter them over the charred area.

"Boy, are you gonna get it," I heard Anne's voice.

I looked up and there she was, leaning over the balcony rail with her head cupped in her two hands. She gave me *her* movie-star smile.

"Anne! I'll do anything if you just don't tell." I continued to hide the black ashes.

"Will you make my bed for a month?"

I looked up at her again. My hands were getting black.

"Can I have the biggest piece of dessert for a year?" she asked.

"That's all you want?" I asked hopefully.

"Yep."

"Deal," I said as Anne kicked some leaves off the balcony.

Dry maple leaves twirled gently down upon my head.

My parents never knew that I nearly torched the house. Hey. Brothers and sisters stick together.

# ～ *Faith* ～

*Faith is the substance of things hoped for,*
the evidence of things not seen.

Hebrews 11:1

# Faith

I have never been to Nebraska, but I believe in its existence, and not just because I've read the atlas, or because I've seen pictures, or because I've heard stories from neighbors. I just have faith that it exists.

When I was a boy I thought that if I was not in a place, that place closed up like an old circus and disappeared, and if I returned, the people would come back, set up their houses and trees like a movie set, and pretend that they had been there all along driving to work, planting beans in the garden, riding bicycles along the sidewalks.

Things do open and close for us along the way: job opportunities, decisions to marry or not to marry. Things are revealed to us, then just as quickly disappear: the new flush of anticipation, delight, or pain; a forecast for sudden rain. But there are some things that just never leave us. I believed there was a rabbit hutch hidden deep in the bramble of the woods behind our house when I was eight, and I believed that this hutch appeared and disappeared whenever I came within ten feet of this little place with shutters, a straw roof, and a door made of birch bark.

I picked up information somehow from my older brother and sister that there existed a place where this rabbit lived. To this day I have not told anyone, but for years I pulled on my exploring boots, adjusted the flashlight, found a stick, and stomped about through the woods in search of the birch-bark door.

I thought, in the beginning, that the rabbit hutch was located in the southeastern section of the woods, because that is where the stream flowed and where there stood an old tree trunk covered with briars and vines, a place suitable for a rabbit and a boy of eight.

For some reason I was also frightened of this section of the woods. Again, I was a good listener when I sat in the kitchen and heard my brother and sister speak about what they found during their own explorations. The trouble was, perhaps, that I selected what I thought was interesting and discarded the rest. I probably heard "tree stump," and "looks like a witch," and "snakes."

There were snakes in the woods, harmless garter snakes, but to me they were Hydras lurking under maple leaves. I didn't really believe there was a witch, but I did know of the famous Russian witch, Baba Yaga, who ate children, so just to be sure I always carried a stick. In my mind the "tree stump" swirled around myths of snakes and witches, and a subtle notion that briars were claws waiting to reach out and ensnare boys of eight who carried flashlights.

When I finally accepted that the rabbit hutch was not in the southeastern section of the woods, I formed a plan. If I walked up and down the entire length of the woods and moved sideways each time I reached an end, I would eventually find the rabbit's home because I would have covered every inch of the unexplored land. I found an automobile tire, four mushrooms, a jack-in-the-pulpit, a junkyard filled with glass bottles and rusted cans, a golf ball, a shoe, and my cat sitting on a rock waiting for me. I did not find the rabbit's place.

After a number of years I gave up the hunt, but to this day I believe there is a comfortable rabbit in a tunic, eating green beans and carrots, lolling on his bed in his house made of straw and birch bark. I've never seen it, but I know it is there, like Nebraska and faith and mushrooms.

The hunt is far more rewarding than the discovery, for during the journey there is anticipation, a sense of purpose, an idea that we are going somewhere, filling in the time, doing something worthwhile.

That I never found the rabbit's hutch still gives me a moment's pause of delight, still temps me to pull on my exploring boots and fish around in search of a flashlight.

# Faith in Goodness

❧

I am not very good with my hands. I type with two fingers. I cannot draw. I fumble baseballs. I am not able to cut a straight line with a saw. A century ago it was essential that fathers and mothers handed down to their children the needed knowledge and skills to survive. I have often said that I wished I knew something about farming, or engines, or leather, or fishing, something I could teach my sons and daughter how to do with the use of their hands. The only thing I directly taught one of my children while exhibiting the dexterity of my fingers was how to make a knot for a necktie.

My oldest son, David, was on his way to a spring dance in his freshman year in high school, a semi-formal affair. He and his mother shopped for a shirt. David borrowed my shoes, and he had a pair of dark pants, leftovers from eighth-grade graduation the year before.

"Dad, I need help with this tie."

I felt like a magician, a surgeon, an artisan of knots and haberdashery. David was a fifteen-year-old boy who just wanted a tie. After I tried to show him how to make the two ends even, I gave up, looped the tie around my own neck, loosened the knot, slipped the tie over my head, and handed it to my son. The dance was a success.

# Faith

Why is it that some people are good with their hands,
capable of poking the thread through the needle, able to draw
a rose more rose-like than the original, while other people,
well, they just do the best they can?

My neighbor's daughter Lisa underwent a liver transplant
last year. She was suddenly ill, and suddenly at the top of the
list for a donor. We take for granted such a transplant. We
ought to gape as we watch what surgeons do each day. A
worker fell from a construction site, died, and his liver was
flown two hundred miles so that it could be placed into the
body of a brave, sick girl.

I looked out my window yesterday and notice Lisa returning
home from school: her backpack slung over her shoulder, her
hair tied in the back, her black shoes pressing against the dark
street. She saw me writing here at my desk and waved. I
waved too.

What do you see out the window? Just a girl walking home,
or a miracle, motion suspended, unobserved simplicity, the
texture of the cloth in her sack, the curve to her hair. To me,
Lisa is a walking miracle destined for a long life with a liver
that people sewed inside her. Some people manipulated an
object with their hands, and a child walked out of the hospital
with a future. Is it magic? I know magic.

Two weeks before Christmas my wife and I brought our
children to the FAO Schwartz toy store in Manhattan. We let
them freely lead the way among the giant stuffed animals and
precise train sets. As we maneuvered around a stack of board
games, we came upon a salesman behind a green counter
performing various magic tricks: a match floating above a
playing card, a stack of quarters appearing and disappearing
under a gold cylinder, diamonds invisibly leaping from paddle
to paddle in the hands of the quick magician.

Michael's nose just reached the tall counter that was covered in deep green velvet. Each time the man moved his

hands, my son's eyes widened. Even I asked, "How'd you do that?" Of course the reply was that no magician ever reveals his tricks. I bought Michael the floating match stick.

In Egyptian hieroglyphs the hand signifies action. "Ladies and gentlemen, allow me to demonstrate for you here in my hands a liver, a human liver. With a flick of the wrist, it is turned into a stack of quarters, right before your eyes, or a match stick, or the life of a little girl."

This year is over. We've exchanged gifts from hand to hand, linked hands in our churches, held bottles of champagne, earned money, bought and sold goods, caressed those we love, pushed revolving doors.

Yes, in the struggles of our everyday living we see on our televisions and in our newspapers the horror of what our hands are capable of doing, but we also see magic, and Lisa waving with her raised hand as she walks past our open window.

# Faith in the Snow

~

During a sudden infusion of heat from southern winds, I grabbed the rake and work gloves one last time to give the yard a final sweep before the paw of winter extended its claws from the north.

The lawn was moist and soft. If I applied too much pressure with the rake, I extracted grass and roots. Gently, gently I combed the final oak and maple leaves across the yard and into a waiting barrel. I felt ambitious enough to pull the leaves out of the pachysandra. As I brushed my rake over the ground covering, I snagged a small shoe and dragged it out onto the lawn. It was a small red sneaker with a white tip, a sneaker belonging to a boy named David, a three-year-old boy, a boy who now turns seventeen this February, a boy looking at colleges, anticipating the acquisition of his driver's license. I had found my son's sneaker, which he had lost thirteen years ago.

I picked up the shoe and stuffed it in my coat as I continued to rake the leaves. I worked up to the house and cleaned around the garage. As I pulled the garbage cans away from the wall, an insect, a thin, translucent insect, flew out from under a leaf and hovered in the sunlight for a moment. There I was, in mid-November, standing before a summer creature that was, I'm sure, puzzled. It is easy to be spun around, to become dizzy or disoriented.

That evening my youngest son said, "Dad, we have to go to the cemetery. I have to find out when Jacob Manderville died." Michael was working on a school assignment about local history, and he had chosen Jacob Manderville.

"Can't we go tomorrow?" I suggested.

"The paper is due tomorrow. It will only take a second. I know where his grave is." So Michael and I drove to the local cemetery and sure enough we quickly found Jacob Manderville: 1806–1896. As we stepped away from the tombstone, Michael and I realized that we were lost.

"The car is this way," he said.

"No, I think we came in over by those trees."

As we walked around for a few moments, Michael asked, "Are the peoples' bones in the ground?"

"Yes."

"I see the car," Michael said. "I'll beat you there," and he ran off between the tombstones. We weren't lost anymore.

That night I remembered the shoe in my coat pocket and brought it to my wife. "Roe, look what I found in the pachysandra this afternoon. Remember how we looked for this?" And I placed the dirty, small, red sneaker in her hand. She went up to the attic and came down with the other one. I was dazed for a moment. "Could the children have grown that quickly?"

All is in place. The summer insect slipped between a crack in the clapboard, the bones in the cemetery are at peace once again, a pair of sneakers is stored back up in the attic, and winter has roared throughout the neighborhood.

It is snowing.

# Faith in Who We Once Were

◦≫

Most writers have an affinity for the Mad Hatter at Alice's tea party, or they ought to. There is a silliness we assume that can be created with boiled words poured into teacups. "And if you drink," we say to a willing reader, "you might be silly too!"

Perhaps it is not a silliness but a sense of being drunk, or bawdy, or just a bit frightened that the party will soon be over. Such silliness can come upon us at the most unlikely times.

"We will have unseasonably warm weather for the next twenty-four hours," the man on the radio reported in the middle of January. "Warm air will push up from the south. The thermometer could reach as high as sixty degrees." That is silliness in a New Jersey winter.

By the late evening there was an earth smell, a moisture, a rousing creature stirring up from the cold and ice, surely not spring, but a silly man stepping out into the yard with his hands in his pockets leaning back, looking up, disposed to his sense of place and time as he considered a distant light in a clear licorice night when all the stars and moon hung like jewels on the salesman's display board.

With my house to my back, and the children sleeping, and my wife sleeping, and the dog sitting at my side as I reached down to pet her, I heard the small cry of my neighbor's new baby. I saw a single light in her window. Two doors down, I saw another light above a garage and a single moth in a drunken state of false hope hurling itself again and again against the glass lamp.

I remembered other moths, other lights, a place in southern France where I spent, as a teenager, a few weeks with my uncle and aunt and with my three cousins: Anne, Tessy, and Isabelle. We filled the days touring castles and caves, walking the battlements, and seeing painted antelope gallop across the millennia on rock walls. I remember a certain moisture against my arms as we all walked through the caves, and a certain voice shouting as we climbed stone towers and called down to my uncle, "Here we are!" A silliness perhaps.

In the evenings of that summer visit, Isabelle and I climbed the roof of a small barn and simply watched the stars. She was all French and I all English. We both wore blue jeans. I learned the word for star in French, *étoile,* and she just laughed at my accent.
And we laughed some more. I could have asked her to pass me the teakettle.

Once, as we sat on the roof with our flashlights, we found a snail crawling along the slate. When she said "escargot" I laughed at my own silliness, not realizing all along that the pretentious "escargot" of New York City restaurants was once a snail with his house on its back sliding across the European continent. Silly little snail.

There is a panorama to our lives, a sweeping dome, perhaps like the night sky. The dog looked up, perhaps waiting for me to say, "Come on, up with you, to Orion and back! Let's go, you silly dog."

Perhaps we could fly over the clothesline toward the Milky Way. But no, the dog just wanted a reassuring pat on its head.

Ask a little boy to step out in the yard. What will he see? Trees, the moon perhaps, a neighbor's house, and that is all.

# Faith

Ask a man in his forties what he sees and he might say the constellation Escargot.

Just before I returned to the house, I noticed a slight movement across the small patch of grass that defines the yard. Under the garden shed something. The dog noticed it too. She stood up. I strained my eyes. A shadow, a motion, a suggestion of life and seriousness and then a skunk. It too recognized the welcome heat from the south, this skunk taking advantage of a sudden memory of grubs and heat and summer nights filled with crickets and moonlight.

The dog ran across the yard before I had a chance to hold her back. The skunk quickly stood on its front legs and sent the dog howling toward the back door. The smell! The barking! The sudden lights in the house!

"What happened?" my wife asked me as she stood in the kitchen laughing. She too knows of the silliness. "What's that smell?"

"The dog, she went after a skunk."

The children thought it was wonderful. I used two cans of tomato juice to bathe the dog. What could be sillier than a man bathing a dog in tomato juice?

The following night my family was once again asleep. The dog was asleep. I stepped out into the yard again. The temperature had dipped back to the serious low teens. The neighbor's baby was asleep. No wild moth. The skunk probably curled itself back in a nest of leaves under the shed dreaming of a warm night and a wild dog, and I thought about a slate roof and a French girl as I leaned against the house.

We all, writers and readers and dreamers, continue to make our own way across the continent of our serious lives under the eye of the laughing moon and under the light of each silly star.

# Faith in the Routine

⌒

I am surrounded by stillness: The clay Chinese horseman sits stiffly on my bookshelf. The framed images of my family do not move in the photographs that hang on the wall. Dried wheat in the bottle on my desk does not bend to a spring breeze, for there is no breeze in this room where I write, and winter holds trees and grass in the grip of cold outside my window.

I like to observe things in motion: the sparrow turning its head as it sits on a thin forsythia branch, a woman brushing a bit of hair away from her face, a kite with a gust of wind pulling it higher and higher over the holiday beach. But then the bird is suddenly gone and the bush is still, the kite is carried home, and the sky is empty. The woman disappears back into her house or into my lost imagination.

We labor at the tasks of a daily routine, and in such labor arms, muscles, heart, blood work in unison to build a house, return a phone call, write a report. In my room, only my body moves, but the observer cannot observe self and then paint or write or dream. It is by sitting back on the lawn chair, as the sun illuminates field and grass and distant geese flying overhead, that a person can give shape to what glides across the imagination.

# Faith

Yesterday, as I sat down at my desk to write, there was a sudden commotion outside my window. One red pickup truck, and then another and another. Seven red pickup trucks appeared on the street. Men with hats and work gloves stepped out of these trucks. A backhoe lumbered and bounced into view, and a dump truck roared around the bend and stopped in the middle of the street.

For the past many years our street has flooded during severe storms. Each time there has been a significant amount of rain, a pool, a lake, a near ocean formed along the road's surface, the grass, the neighbor's walk. Yesterday, the town's department of public works decided enough is enough: the ocean must be drained.

All day the men stooped to their labor, opening storm drains, cutting into the road, digging a deep trench, pouring stones into the hole. They could have been pirates or under the employ of Jules Verne.

There was much talk and laughter while the backhoe clawed at the dirt. Men drove machines, scooped up stones with their shovels, jumped into the trench and dug some more. Trucks drove in and out of the street.

By late afternoon they were all gone, those men and their trucks. The open ditch was filled with stones and earth. Each house and tree sat still in its usual place. I was pleased to drive to the school and see my children walking toward me as they waved in greeting and shambled and bumbled and rolled into the car with their day stories. My daughter brushed the hair away from her face. My son swung his backpack onto the seat. The movement of my children, their arms and legs, their smiles and laughter, pleased me.

I am reading a book about island biology and how plants and animals often develop differently in these remote bits of land created by volcanic eruptions or quirks of land separation from the various continents. People discovered elephant bones on these islands, so biologists assumed that some of the islands were once connected by land bridges to the continents, for how else to explain the elephants? But then other biologists observed that if there were land bridges, there ought to be evidence of other large animals on the islands, such as tigers and lions, but there was not.

It is suggested that elephants swam to the islands. Elephants swim! I was pleased to read this, pleased to learn that something as big and slow and gray as stone could swim. They must kick into the water and float at the same time. Could they, perhaps, paddle with their ears, or float in the sky attached to a string? No matter, the movement of elephants in the water is an image of delight and odd grace.

It has been reported that people have seen the tip of an elephant's truck poking out from under the sea water and the hump of its back breaking the surface as it makes its way kicking from underneath its weight.

As I write, the elephant too sinks into my dreams, the movement stilled, and I lean back in my chair, and the chair creaks under my weight, and the hands of the pine Shaker clock to my right have moved around the flat surface of the clock's face, but I did not notice.

There has been the quick exchange of blood and oxygen in my body. My fingers click-clacked against the keys where I type, but at the day's end the red town trucks are parked over at the municipal garage, the children are sleeping in their beds, the sparrow sleeps like a stone in the cold winter night, and the fossils of elephant bones are held fast in the island history.

We move to the sound of those we love, to the call of our labor, to the heave of breath billowing inside our chests. The geese, look at the geese flying overhead! And can you imagine elephants swimming across the Ganges River?

All, all eventually returns to stillness. I closed my writing room for the night, arranged my papers in order, and turned off the light. I looked out my window and up into the quiet sky. I ran my two hands against my cheeks, and then I saw the moon swimming out toward what, an island, a place of grass and air and sun where pirates swim with elephants?

Where is the water that accumulated in my street? Down, down in the new silent drain. Good night. Good night. We sink in the stillness of a forgiving sea.

# Faith in What Is Lost

∾

We are accustomed to pleasure and the knowledge that such pleasure can be repeated: going to the movies, eating, listening to music, welcoming spring's sudden heat. But what of the experience that is pleasurable and will never be experienced again? How do we respond when we know such experience is a single instance in our lives even while we are going through the moments of pleasure?

The first book that I purposely read slowly to savor the joy was Rainer Maria Rilke's *Letters to a Young Poet*. I knew, for the first time in my life, that a book could hold a charmed promise of some hidden pleasure when I began to read Rilke's correspondence with the aspiring writer. I did not know at the time that I would someday be a writer, but I knew, when Rilke said "love your solitude and bear with sweet-sounding lamentation the suffering it causes you," that I was experiencing a pleasure that I could not repeat. When I finish reading a book that I love, I soon hunger for that feeling again, but I cannot recreate the exact feeling by simply rereading the book. So I read Rilke slowly, over a period of a week. Each night I propped my head on my pillow, opened the book to the marker I had left between the pages, and continued to read and listen and feel and understand.

# Faith

Often, when I am invited to give a talk, I feel this sense of living a moment that cannot be repeated. To fly across the country, to descend through the clouds and into a California airport, to be driven two more hours in a car to a small village and to be asked to speak about writing or loneliness or memories or action is, as all true writers know, a humbling experience. No writer of worth goes before an audience believing what he or she has to say is unique. The true writer simply recapitulates what everyone in the audience already knows and feels.

A writer confirms a loss and love in the reader, that is all. There are people who write books and who give talks simply for the money, and often for their own egos. Of course it is pleasing to be the center of attention in an auditorium or in the book-review section of a newspaper, and the more a person likes that feeling, the more he or she steps away from what it is that makes someone worth listening to.

To stand before a crowd and read something I've written is a moment that cannot be relived, for the people are different, the notion of the moment is different. Often when I am being driven back to the airport I say to myself, "I will never see this little village again in my life. Let me remember something of this place." And I look for an image, a tree, children playing in a yard, a colorful garden of flowers and laundry .

To know that we are living a unique experience not to be lived again gives us a sense of immediate contemplation. To see a school of dolphin leap out of the water on the morning of a summer holiday brings an immediate shout of glee from my children. The discovery of the purple crocuses once again exploding in the garden brings my son charging into the house with the flowers in his raised hand and a confirmation: "Look!"

We all recognize this state of contemplation at the end of something: graduation, the death of a friend, the moving out of a house, the end of a job or time spent in a particular place.

All these things create in us an urge to remember, to gather various memories and sigh or weep or hold within the feelings that twirl around our minds and hearts for a future that can only be guessed at. We savor delights, look forward to vacations, take pictures of things that impress us so that we will remember.

The forecast for this afternoon calls for snow. I begin my day here in this small room where I begin to write at 8:00 and write until noon. We've had a mild winter with little snow, so I look forward to sitting here as the snow falls all around me. I am surrounded by three windows: east, south, west. The sun rolls around me throughout the day. In the morning I write. In the afternoon I send out letters or make phone calls. This afternoon it will snow, and I will not write letters or use the phone. Instead, I plan to listen to Aaron Copland's "Appalachian Spring" and write some poetry and look out the window to my right and see the yard and neighborhood turn into something different from what they usually are, and I will look as the fence and trees and bushes and houses change color and shape and all will ask for a new explanation, all will be seen in a new way. I will open the window and reach out to a bush and scoop a bit of snow onto my hand and lick the snow and let it melt on my tongue. I will relish the cold feeling and sense my loneliness. I will close my window and know that winter is almost over.

The snow will recede, back into the hidden ways of nature, and I know that spring is three weeks away, and I have been through forty-five spring seasons, and I can anticipate the pleasure of another spring, but now I know that it is not just one winter, one bit of snow on my tongue, one adventure that I see that will not last. It is all, all a single life, our lives, the whole not the part, that is lived once. Yes, we can repeat a pleasure from week to week. We can return to a certain summer vacation spot and relive the joy of last year. We can return to those we love and surrender ourselves to the pleasure of a hand against our back and feel the supple movements of love and pleasure. But I also know that our lives are a collection of joys and sorrows, each one lived in a different way each time, though it may appear that the experiences are similar.

A writer who captures the moment of joy and sorrow in words that can be relived again and again is a writer to invite across the country for a speaking engagement. But remember, it is not the writer you wish to hear, but your own voice mouthing the words, your own heart feeling the ache, your own roots deeply planted in the garden of contemplation that bears flowers when you are lonely and in need of personal renewal.

# Faith in Self

$\sim$

Last night I had a terrible dream. I was alone in the house where I grew up with my brother Oliver, blind, mute, crippled, vacuous Oliver, who was in his bed for thirty-two years incapable of doing or learning anything.

I was downstairs in the living room playing marbles on the carpet when I felt a sudden ache, a deeply felt sense of guilt and anguish. I had forgotten to feed my brother.

As I woke up from my dream, horrified that Oliver was hungry, I looked to my left and right only to realize that I was in my own home, with my own family, and Oliver had died seventeen years ago today on March 12, 1980.

In this room where I write I have a Shaker clock ticking peacefully against one wall. A plane is flying overhead at this very moment. This morning, while doing the breakfast dishes, I noticed a slight piece of jam on a red bowl I was washing. I thought to myself that I could easily leave that small dot of jam on the bowl and no one would notice, no one would care that I didn't clean the bowl perfectly, but then I gave the bowl an extra swipe with my blue sponge and placed the bowl in the rack to dry.

Who cares about clocks ticking, or spots of jam, or an airplane zooming over the house? When the astronauts circle around us in space, they could easily think about holding the globe in their outstretched palms, a single ball of blue and white. From a distance it is difficult to see the swirls and colors that make up the whole picture.

I visited the Chicago Art Museum recently for an exhibition of Degas's work, his paintings, drawings, and sculptures. I was pleased and disturbed to see, on close examination, that his famous dancers and bathers were marks made with brush and paint. My pleasure arose with the thought that beauty can be created, a living beauty that evokes passion and simplicity, and my turbulence came from the realization that such beauty is just an image, something framed, displayed, but not held.

No matter how hard I willed my brother Oliver to stand up and run in the yard with me when I was a boy, he didn't, yet I didn't find it difficult to reconcile his disabilities with the sense that he was a real person after all, not a wooden Pinocchio.

I remember leaning over Oliver's bed and staring into his eyes, almost nose to nose, for I wanted to see if he was really blind. He was, of course, but his eyes looked just like mine. Even though Oliver could not hold anything or pick up anything, his hands looked just like my hands. I watched as my mother clipped his fingernails. Real fingernails, just like mine.

The only way Oliver could drink was if someone held his head up from the pillow and placed the rim of a glass at the tip of his lips, then he would drink, just like I drank. I could see his throat muscles work the liquid down into his body.

I look at my Shaker clock and know it tells time just as well as my son's digital clock in his bedroom. I listen to the plane flying overhead and think of the physics of flight, which lifts everything that flies: jets and space crafts; loons and butter-flies.

We see, each day, bits of things that represent the whole. A jam spot on a bowl in the morning represents everything that we do or don't do: clean the bowl as best we can, even though no one is looking, or let the small spot go for, again, no one is looking and who would care if the job wasn't finished as best we could?

A man with a brush, a canvas, and young women didn't end up painting *Dancer with Bouquets*, or *The Millinery Shop*, or *Nude Woman Drying Herself*. Degas wiped away the spot of jam, listened to the clock ticking, and he remembered to feed Oliver.

# Faith in Marriage

In one of his lectures my college philosophy professor said, "A man who does not have contemplation cannot yet enjoy the adornment of sun, moon, and stars. For there is need of the apparition of *a woman clothed with the sun, and having the moon under her feet, and upon her head a crown of twelve stars* (Ap. 12.1)."

I liked that so much I wrote it in my notebook. I was a lonely young man when I was in college, longing for a woman whom I could love and who could love me. I saw plenty of apparitions, but none clothed with the sun and the moon and with a crown of twelve stars, and I did not have any sense of contemplation when I was nineteen years old.

When I returned to my college dorm one afternoon after class, some friends, whom I'll call Jason, Brian, and JD, were listening to the music of Crosby, Stills, Nash, and Young. The stereo screamed around the room. Jason and Brian were smoking a joint. JD smiled with his eyes as I stepped into the room.

"Hello, Chrissy," Jason said as offered me what he was smoking.

"I'm not interested," I said with the confidence of a mouse in a snake pit.

Jason looked at me, my hair, my lumpy sweater, my tight jeans, my worn shoes. "You need an education," he said as he turned to Brian and JD. They both laughed.

"We're on our way to a river party," Brian said as he stepped up to me and blew smoke into my eyes, "the first one of the year. We'd like you to come."

I looked at Jason and JD and back to Jason. "Well, I've already made plans for tonight."

"Chrissy, *boy*," Jason said, heavily accenting the word *boy*, "you don't seem to get this. A party, an invitation-only party. Are you coming?"

It was hard to make a definite judgment. I understood the tribe mentality: camaraderie, initiation, a sense of joining so that all are not threatened.

"Yeah, count me in."

Jason inhaled deeply. Brian turned the stereo up. JD dropped his tongue out from his mouth, let it hang loosely as he shook his head back and forth, rolled his tongue back into his mouth, then screamed, "Party!" I shook my head up and down a bit to the rhythm of "Suite: Judy Blue Eyes."

Jason and Brian left the room and returned within minutes with blankets and a cooler. JD pulled out an extra blanket from under his bed and one from the closet. "Here. You might need this," he said as he tossed a blanket toward me. Eagles fly. Dolphins swim. Young men seek rapture at the bottom of a wine bottle, floating with a woman wrapped in a blanket, or so I discovered at the river.

Kelly was already waiting for us with three other girls under the bridge. The bridge was a double-lane highway crossing the river, built during the depression under the WPA. When I read the plaque that was bolted to the first pillar of concrete, I tripped. I tried to reach out and grab the pillar, but instead I missed and my hand raked against the rusted plaque. The nail on my right index finger caught the edge of the plaque and tore from my finger. The nail hung from my bleeding hand. I didn't dare pull the nail off completely because it hurt a great deal as it was. I quickly stood up, pretending nothing happened. No one noticed.

As we stepped over loose stones and bramble, balancing our bodies through the slow descent to the bank, I helped Jason with the cooler. Brian slipped and slid to the river side. Everyone laughed. JD galloped and was the first one to meet the girls, townies, as they were called, girls who graduated from high school, worked in local stores and factories, girls who knew the difference between boredom and salvation. The problem was they sought salvation on Friday nights under a bridge wrapped in blankets with Christian boys who knew the difference between a wet river and a dry river. The problem was that they never knew, and probably never learned that no matter how much the river flows into the ocean, the ocean is never full. In their constant need to fill the dry river they didn't drink the water, tend to the silver water, ply the water with their hands in humility and love. Rather, they just wanted to get drunk, toss empty wine bottles into the river, surrender themselves to the darkness in the blankets and laugh and laugh. For there was much laughter when I was introduced to Kelly and her friends. They all knew I was the freshman, the new kid, the one to be encouraged.

As we stood under the bridge, Jason and Brian dipped the cooler into the water and pulled out four bottles of wine, one for each couple: Jason and Kelly, Brian and Brenda, a girl who looked like an A&P checkout girl and a princess, and JD and Tisha, a girl who claimed to be the cousin of a U.S. Congressman. I was introduced to Linda, a dark-haired, dark-eyed girl who still wore her high school ring and spoke in whispers. "I'm new too, but I thought it might be fun."

"I know fun," I said as I looked at Linda. She started to unbutton the top of her blouse. I turned to look for Jason and the others, but they had already disappeared into the tall grass that lined the river. My finger throbbed.

"Ah," I said. "Do you want to, ah . . . "

"We can sit down. Did you bring a blanket?" Linda asked, as she too walked toward the grass.

"Yeah. Sure." I stepped back to where the cooler was and found the last blanket, the one Brian had given me. I stepped over to where Linda was sitting. She had opened all the buttons on her shirt. She wasn't wearing a bra. I spread the blanket out and crushed the grass underneath. Linda took a long drink from the wine and waited.

"I'll be just a minute," I said, as I stepped back into the darkness. I could hear much laughter and whispers in various places in the grass beyond where Linda sat. I stepped backward again a bit, and a bit more, and a bit more, until I started climbing up the embankment. By the time I reached up and touched the WPA plaque, I could hear, in the distance, Jason calling out "Chrissy! Where the hell'd you go?" I heard Linda swearing at Kelly, "Now what am I supposed to do?" And I heard Brian say, "You could join us," and then there was much laughter, and I ran and ran.

If I had had a black hat and big shoes and a thin cane, I would have looked like Charlie Chaplin, the man-child running away through the dark woods back to the campus that was illuminated like a birthday cake. Instead, I was a nineteen-year-old boy with a bleeding finger, which I sucked. I was a person unaware that the seminal reason of our existence can be found hidden within ourselves, our peculiar selves born among the circumstance of our living and among the gifts we were given. It is, so I have learned, the combination of circumstance and free will that makes a person whole. We must live the circumstance and act upon the circumstances. In the act we are so defined. At the time, all I knew was that my finger hurt. I didn't know about living a courageous life. I just wanted to be in love with a woman, so I ran away from the river. The night was warm, the stars were freely displayed against the arch of the universe.

I did not know that I would be married six years later, that Roe and I would be married for twenty years, that we would have three children, but running away from the river that night I hoped that someday Roe would be there, my Roe, *clothed with the sun, and having the moon under her feet, and upon her head a crown of twelve stars.*

# Faith in God

❧

Do you believe in the light of God? We can see, from our mind and from science, that the light God provides is good. Such light allows us to see physically and brings us a certain truth about our behavior and how we express ourselves. The poets know of such expression and light. The condemned man is the man without faith. Such a man creates a cave for himself where he cannot see his own reflection or his own shadows. We must be able to see who we are and see how we project ourselves upon the world in order to define who we are. Without the light of faith, we are plunged into darkness. Many people call such darkness loneliness. They are alone who do not have faith.

What do we seek? What do we seek? Much of the world is in turmoil. We divide the wealthy from the poor, we condemn the weakest among us as burdens, the issue of race will destroy us. What is it that we seek?

Love. Yes, love. Exactly that. Love is what we seek, and such love is possible in the reunion of the body and soul. We must understand that our fears are holy, that our sorrow is just, that our joy is pure and true and, above all else, we must trust. We cannot see most of what I speak, but such vision belongs to those who deserve such light, who dare to reach out and touch such light, not the light of fire, but the light of who they are in union with another human being. We cannot have this light delivered to us in a package from the department store. Such light comes to us through the grace of God.

In Romans, chapter 8, verse 18, it is written, *The sufferings of the present time are not worthy to be compared to the glory to come.* We will become ill if we are deprived of this disposition, this affective disposition. What heals? What heals? Not the physician. What heals us from the disease of fear and sorrow, from darkness born out of darkness? What cure, what passion, what state to lure us back, back toward the light? How to purge the infection? Physician, heal thyself and the medicine is the grace of God, the physician God. *Neither herb nor application cured them, but Your all-healing Word, O Lord!* And what is the word of God but the Bible old and new, the Son of God, the prophets, and the lilies of the field.

Do we have the wings of ostriches? It is faith in God, the God who must be satisfied, that propels us. Faith heals. Faith straightens. Faith alone divides the light from the darkness. Romans 13:12: *"The night is far advanced; the day is at hand. Let us therefore put on the armor of light."*

The armor of light, my dear children, is the embrace of those who love us and the embrace of God. Without the embrace, there is darkness. Without the light of the embrace, there is the darkness that will cover us. Let us cover ourselves with the hands of those who love us, and with the hand of God upon our forehead.

# Faith in the Moon

☙

I will tell you this: I am attracted to the moon, and I admit I think of it as something female, like the ocean, which is also a natural symbol for femininity: powerful, moist, advancing and receding in a cycle that mystifies and attracts attention. But the ocean is seventy-five miles from where I live. The moon is a regular visitor.

Often, when I pick up Michael from a late Little League baseball practice, or I drive Karen home from a friend's house in the early evening, the face of the full moon rises in the east through the trees. It dominates the dark horizon, a sand dollar on the beach of the universe, a silver quarter to pocket, a token to remind me that what is beautiful is often out of reach but to be cherished just the same.

We touched the blue surface of the round moon with a rocket ship, walked against the surface, stirred up the dust, recorded photographs of a barren terrain marred with craters.

My moon slides into my room at night through the small crack between the shade and the window sill. Sometimes she sits on my bed, or illuminates the wall with a straight line, light from the sun, they say, reflected from the moon, sent back to earth and reflected once again against my wall and into my tired eyes, but I say pearl-fire, moon-honey, straw turned to gold on the spinning-wheel moon.

# Faith

Driving home one evening from my parents' house, Michael concluded, "Hey, the moon is following us," for it seemed, as we drove through little towns, under trees, past diners and movie theaters, that the moon leaped over mountains, weaved through treetops, kept up with us as we drove along the highway. The moon, to an eight-year-old boy, contains its own propulsion, charting her own path from one house to the next. When I carried Michael to bed, he looked out the window and said, "It stopped right over the house."

How do I say to a boy that the moon protects us, that his mother is the moon? A father might be the sun according to myths, the father might be the wheel or the stag striking the earth with a hoof, but the moon, she appears and disappears, following us, keeping track, surrounding us at night with a protective shawl, a lunar embrace men cannot give, but need in order to survive.

One of the best attractions in Washington, D.C. is the National Air and Space Museum. Charles Lindbergh's *Spirit of St. Louis* hangs from the ceiling; actual Apollo space capsules sit on display; and just as you enter the large building, there is a small slice of the moon, a bit of moon rock that everyone is allowed to touch. I remember holding a few Belgian coins in my hand after my grandfather emptied his pockets after we picked him and my grandmother up from the airport. Coins from Belgium!

To touch a bit of the moon at the museum, to run my fingertip along the smooth piece of stone, is to rub against the cheek of my mother, the earth of me under the watchful eye. A coin from the universe!

For centuries there have been virulent arguments about the center of the universe: the earth is the center, the sun is the center, man is the center, Rome is the center, Paris is the center. I step out into the yard at night and welcome the moon that sits between the tree branches, little moon, Cheshire Cat with a smile, goddess, Chinese lantern, and I think of the women I love, and remember the embrace. I am no Galileo, but I suspect that the moon is the center of the universe, the moon of Eve, the moon in a goose nest, the moon of silk, the moon at my window tapping on the glass, kissing the glass, penetrating the glass, illuminating my bedroom at night, the glow of the moon, the flowers of the moon, a bit of ivory, a fan made from rice paper, the cheek of night, the tomb of light. I see the moon, and the moon sees me. God bless the moon, and God bless me.

# Faith in Prayer

⤳

I didn't pray much as a child. I didn't know that prayer made a difference. Now I've discovered prayer because I am alone. I am surrounded by my wife and children, by my friends and by professional people, but now, as an adult, I realize that I am alone.

Sometimes when I pray I try to hear what God is saying back to me. As a writer I often receive letters from my readers: a beautiful handwritten note from California wishing me well, or a typed letter from Maine that includes a few words of encouragement or gratitude. I wrote an essay once about a trip I took to Vermont. I wrote an incidental remark about the beauty of birch trees, and how I felt that I could crawl right inside the middle of a birch tree and just discover my soul there. For some reason this woman wrote to me about birch trees. My article was over four thousand words. The part about the birch trees was, perhaps, two sentences, and yet that is what she wrote about, and how grateful she was to discover someone else felt the same way about birch trees.

When I stop writing, I suppose I will stop receiving letters like that. It seems to make sense that when I pray, I hope to hear God answering me back, even if it is about something incidental. I often pray to God for a peaceful heart. This is not an easy thing to acquire, but I think, perhaps, birches have something to do with it.

Now that I take a backward look I realize at what time my life began to be divided between time past and time future. We never know what event is the first motion that moves the rest of our lives to a new point of growth. To grow is to endure pain, for such pain involves the loss of what has been inside of us.

If I had to say when I began to receive hints of loneliness, hints of a world beyond my own childhood, hints that I might need to pray, I would probably have to say it was the day that part of the elephant tree died.

In the backyard of the house where I lived as a child there was an apple tree about the size of a bus, except it didn't look like a bus: it looked like an elephant. The trunk of the tree (which didn't look like the trunk of an elephant) was thick, thicker than an elephant's leg, but I pretended it was an elephant's leg. Well, that's not the part of the tree that looked like an elephant. The part that looked like an elephant was the thick branch that spread up like an elephant's trunk sniffing for a peanut.

In those days, when I visited a zoo, I reached out over the fence, where they say don't feed the animals, and I stretched out with a peanut in my hand. You have to know what rules to break when you are a child.

The elephant at the zoo lived in a pit. I remember looking down and seeing the elephant walking in and out of a brown pool of water.

I always felt sorry for the elephant because it lived by itself. When I waved a peanut back and forth and said, "Bo! Here Bo!," the elephant lifted his trunk in a question-mark shape, poked his nostrils through the fence, sniffed the peanut, then pulled it right out of my hand.

I liked listening to the elephant's snorting sound. I made that sound sometimes when I popped my head out of the water at the town pool in the summer just at the exact same time my sister Maria popped out from the water. I wanted to scare her, but she would just shake her head back and forth trying to get the water to drain from her ears while I stuck my nose and mouth into the water, then I blew and screamed at the same time. The lifeguards didn't like it because they thought I was hurt. It was against the rules to pretend you were in need of help.

Well, the branch in the apple tree looked just like the elephant's trunk trying to reach the peanut in my hand.

Another part of the tree that looked like an elephant was the saddle, right where the tree made a V shape.

One afternoon I slung a piece of rope under the branch, sat in the saddle, and began to ride my elephant tree to Alaska. I read that summer about Hannibal and how, while riding elephants, he vanquished his enemies in a sneak attack over the snow-covered Alps, so it always seemed to me that I ought to ride my elephant in the snow. I always thought elephants belonged in jungles, so when I read that elephants were used in the winter, I thought that was funny. It's like thinking about pumpkins hanging on a Christmas tree.

My trip to Alaska took the whole afternoon. The danger increased as we started walking along the narrow side of the mountain. The elephant shook and jumped. His ears bounced up and down. His tail whipped back and forth until there was a loud *CRACK,* and the elephant's trunk broke off. That is when my grandfather stepped out on the porch.

"Boy!" my grandfather yelled. My grandfather never talked to me; he always yelled, or it seemed that way, especially when I wasn't doing what he wanted, or what he expected.

"Boy! What have you done?" He stood at the top of the porch stairs and looked across the orange day lilies. I was flat on the ground, nearly eating grass as the broken tree branch squashed my leg.

"Bon Papa!" I called out. *Bon papa* is French for "good father." I was never sure why we called him that. I didn't think that he was good, and he wasn't my father, but it seemed to fit him just the same, like the word *grapefruit*. I never understood how a fruit that big and that yellow could have gotten the word *grape* in its name, but it seemed to fit somehow.

"Bon Papa!" I yelled again. "I'm here! Under the tree!"

Things must have looked funny from his point of view. The last time he was in the garden, before lunch, the yard was in order: the flowers were blooming, the lawn had been cut, the apple tree stood contentedly in the middle of the property. But now, after lunch, the tree was lopsided, and a ten-year-old boy was pinned under a branch like a fly stuck on a pin.

I watched my grandfather walked down the wooden steps of the porch. He stopped and squinted in the sunlight. I could see his wrinkled face. The lines around his eyes were not the lines of a smile.

"Monster!" my grandfather screamed as he saw me under the tree. I had hoped that he was referring to the crazed apple tree that had turned into a mad elephant that was trying to trample his grandson. "Monster!" my grandfather yelled again as he stomped down the stone stairs leading to the tree. "How many times have I told you to stay out of that tree?!"

I knew who the monster really was. I tried to move my leg, but it was held under the weight of the branch. I thought perhaps I'd try crying, but Hannibal never cried when he was stuck under one of his elephants, so I just waited for my uncertain rescue. That is when I saw my grandmother stepping out on the porch. She began waving her yellow handkerchief. I spit out some grass and waved back.

"Boy, don't move," my grandfather ordered as be tried to lift the branch off my leg. "I need a saw. Wait right here."

As he turned to head in the direction of the garden shed, I began to laugh. He turned on his heels. "What is so funny?"

# Faith

"'Wait right here,' you said, Bon Papa. Get it? 'Wait right here,'" I nodded my head in the direction of the dead elephant squashing my leg.

I distinctly heard him whisper "monster" as he turned again and walked away in pursuit of a saw as my grandmother creaked her way down the garden path and stood over me reciting a prayer in French.

"Baba," I said. I never knew why we called my grandmother Baba. We just did. There is a famous story about Baba Yaga, a witch who lived deep in the woods of Russia and who liked to eat children. My grandmother was an angel and she liked chocolate cake.

"Baba," I said again. "I'm okay." Then she looked at the tree and kicked the broken branch. "Filthy tree," she mum—bled.

At the beginning of the war, when the Nazi troops invaded Belgium, there was a loud pounding on the front door to my grandparents' house. Bon Papa was already in a Spanish prisoner-of-war camp, but my grandmother didn't know that at the time. The SS officers demanded, "Where is the General?" My grandmother looked at them, raised a shaking fist in their faces, and cleverly said, "I hope you find that bum. He ran off with a red-lipped woman a year ago and I never saw him again. He's dirt." The soldiers in black uniforms laughed and never returned to the house.

Two years later, while listening to her hidden, illegal radio, my grandmother heard Bon Papa's voice from England encouraging the underground to continue its fight against Hitler. And two years after that they were finally reunited.

"He'll be out in a second," my grandfather growled to my grandmother on his return trip from the garden shed with a Swedish bow saw in his right hand. A bow saw has the teeth of a shark. I felt as if my leg was dangling in the ocean, dripping blood, waiting to be bitten off.

Bon Papa leaned into the task and began cutting. *Zooba! Zooba! Zooba!* The saw rocked back and forth against the branch. *Zooba! Zooba! Zooba!* Suddenly my grandmother was spinning around the tree. *Zooba! Zooba! Zooba!* My grandfather seemed to expand like a balloon. *Zooba! Zooba! Zooba!* I fainted.

When I woke up in my bed, I prayed that the doctor would not cut off my leg. He didn't. I prayed that my grandfather would forgive me for breaking the branch of his apple tree. He did. And I prayed that someday, when I was a father or grandfather, that I, too, would care as much as my grandfather cared for me, for when I woke up in my bed I saw my grandfather leaning over me a bit. He was crying.

Prayer is connected to loneliness. When we are in need, when we are faced with the possible loss of someone, when we are afraid, we ask God for companionship, or for the restoration of companionship. All it takes to be connected is to write a letter, or to pray. In both cases there will be a response.

# Faith in the Turtle

⟋⟍

The dullness of routine can cripple the soul: the clanking of the kitchen plates, the neighbor chasing after her loose dog, the sun rising in the east and sliding down the same place each night. Sometimes, though, the storm of the unexpected erupts on the calm plain of our existence.

"There's a turtle in the yard! There's a turtle in the yard!" I yelled as I pushed open the kitchen door. If we had a bell in the house when I was eight I would have rushed to the long rope and clamored along with the tolling peal: "A turtle in the yard!"

My mother and father looked up passively from their newspapers and coffee. "But there's a turtle in the garden!" I said.

My mother smiled, stood up from her chair, reached out for my hand and said quietly, "Show me the turtle, Christopher."

I led her past the kitchen table as my father turned the page of his newspaper, led her out the kitchen door to the porch, led her across the gray floor and wood stairs and down into the garden.

"Where is the turtle?" my mother asked with ease and mild interest.

"Over here! Eating the lettuce!"

I pulled on my mother's hand as I brought her to the small lettuce garden my father planted each year. "Over here in the lettuce! You must see!"

I pointed, and my mother gasped. "Oh, my goodness! Call your father quickly. Call your father!"

I ran back up the porch stairs and yelled "Daddy! Come see! Mom wants you to see!"

When my father walked out onto the porch with the wrinkled newspaper in hand, my mother and I were both pointing toward the lettuce garden.

"I've never seen such a thing before," my father said as he tossed the newspaper on a lawn chair and ran down from the porch. There, grinding long lettuce in its mouth, was the biggest turtle I, my mother, and my father had ever seen. It had a large head, a dragon-like tail, claws of a lizard, a shell of a prehistoric nature as round as a manhole. This was a snapping turtle, an old, old snapping turtle, perhaps over a hundred, my father reasoned.

"This *is* a turtle," my mother said as she pulled me closer.

"I'll get the wheelbarrow," my father said as he quickly stepped toward the garage.

We looked at the turtle's eyes. "Can I touch its back?" I asked.

"No, Christopher. It can snap your finger off with its powerful jaws."

I wanted to ride the turtle. It clawed the soil, reached out with its long neck and pulled at a new piece of lettuce, not minding an audience. It was gray and dirty, having come from the swamp beyond the woods and fields. "Such a distance," my mother said. It was on a journey, surely not to find our lettuce, but on its way.

My father returned with the red wheelbarrow, tipped it to the side just at the rim of the turtle's shell; then he took an iron rake and pushed the turtle into the barrow. It sat like a stone, a rock, a heavy load willing to be transported.

"I'll be back in a while. Would you like to come, Christopher?" my father asked.

A boy and his father escorted the great turtle back through the woods, over a distant field, and to the swamp of tall reeds and water. I will always remember how my father brought the turtle to the edge of the wide ditch and slowly, slowly tipped the wheelbarrow until the turtle slid down, down, and splashed into the bog. It quickly lifted its head, then quickly submerged. My father and I watched the turtle swim under the water, under time, under a memory I keep as my father and I walked back through the woods with the empty barrow, back to the garage, back to the porch, back into the house and the newspapers and dinner and fresh lettuce.

What does the poet do between the writing of the poems? What does the boy do between one adventure and the next?

Routine is the glue that keeps the soul attached to the body during our earthly time of duty and ordinary living, preparing us for the turtle's visit.

# Faith When We Are Hungry

❧

Remember what it was like when we first became parents? How we felt in the delivery room, that awe, that love, that moment of deep celebration? That is what a teacher ought to feel when the children enter the classroom each day from September until June. I have met too many teachers and administrators who treat children like empty trash cans that need to be filled with knowledge and wisdom so that they can be turned into flowerpots.

I want to hold the child in my arms like a seed. I want to look at each child who stands before me with reverence and place the spoon of life at the tip of his mouth, and I want to watch him eat and breathe and live and grow and blossom. That is what my mother taught me to do.

One afternoon I was eating lunch in the faculty cafeteria when a guidance counselor entered the crowded room, stepped up to my table, and smiled. I smiled too.

"Chris, could I speak with you in the hallway for a second? I'm sorry to interrupt your lunch."

Ms. Harper and I walked out into the hall, surrounded by eight foot windows. The sun was bathing us with heat. "Chris, we need a home tutor for a boy with muscular dystrophy. He was coming to school for a while in his wheelchair, but now he can't any longer. Would you be interested?" The guidance department knew that I was always interested in home instruction.

"Sure. What day?"

"Well, this is a special case. If you could go twice a week for at least an hour a piece, he could get caught up with his work. He needs to pass English."

"What's his name?"

"Brian Dunn."

After school the next day, I drove across town and looked for the Dunn house, a house number, anything that matched the directions the guidance department secretary had given me. I drove up and down the high-priced neighborhood twice until I stopped and asked a women walking her dog, "Could you tell me where the Dunn's live?"

The woman pointed, "Behind those trees and bushes."

Indeed there was a house behind the tall, overgrown bushes and drooping trees. I turned the car around and drove up to a barely visible driveway that was also surrounded by overgrown plants, vines, bushes. Sticks and leaves scraped against the car as I drove toward a house that once had been beautiful.

I parked the car and walked up to the front door. I rang the bell. Nothing. I rang the bell again. Nothing. Then I noticed a small sign: *Come around back*. I walked to the right, passed the garage, passed the overgrown lawns and ugly garden beds of weeds and rocks. A rusted barbecue grill leaned back against a crumbling wall of cement. I knocked on the door. "Just a minute," a voice emanated from within the dim kitchen.

"Yes?" a woman asked as she opened the door wide.

"I'm Mr. de Vinck. Brian's English tutor?"

"Oh, hello, Mr. de Vinck. It is so good of you to come. I was expecting you." Mrs. Dunn shook my hand warmly as I stepped into her kitchen. There was a smell of cooked brownies. I noticed that every wall in the kitchen, in the distant hallway, and in the living room had a scrape line about three feet from the floor. Wheelchair marks. The house was clean but run down. The windows washed but covered from the outside with overgrown rhododendrons.

"I have a table set up for you in the living room. I'll get Brian." Mrs. Dunn placed a dish of brownies before me. "Help yourself," and then she disappeared down the hallway.

I grabbed a brownie and walked into the living room. On one side sat a large table filled with electronic equipment: radio parts, television screens, tubes, wires. In the middle of the room sat a heavy black lounge chair beside a thin, wood chair. There was a television set, fireplace, pictures of flowers on the wall. I was about to sit in the lounge chair when I heard the whir of a small, electric motor. I turned as Brian spun his wheelchair into the living room, scraping the wall as he moved along. He didn't speak but drove parallel to the low black chair. He looked at me and waited.

"Hello," I said. "I'm Mr. de Vinck, your English teacher."

"Hi," Brian answered, and waited. Then his mother came from the kitchen with a glass of milk. "I thought you'd like to wash down the brownie."

As I drank the cold milk, Mrs. Dunn bent over her son, picked him up, and placed him into the lounge chair, pulled a tube from behind the chair, attached the tube to his nose, adjusted the oxygen tank that stood behind the chair, and then said, "I'll leave you two to your work. If you need anything, I'll be in the kitchen. Sit here, Mr. de Vinck." Mrs. Dunn directed me to the small wood chair. I sat down. She stepped out of the room.

I looked at Brian, his arms and legs as thin as a bird's leg, his face sunken, his eyes huge behind his glasses, his hands skeletal. "Pull my sock up," he ordered.

"The right one or the left?"

"The left."

# Faith

I leaned over and began readjusting his sock, then I turned and asked, "Is that okay?"

He looked at me, and then he spit full-blast into my face. "You're a piece of crap," he said.

As I wiped my face, Brian said, "Pull up my head."

"Are you going to spit again?" I asked.

"Put your hands over my ears, and pull up from there. It will adjust my spine a bit."

I walked behind Brian's chair, stood beside the oxygen tank, leaned over, saw the thick dandruff in his hair, reached down and pulled up Brian's head so that it sat with a better balance upon the ruined pile of his body. "You're a piece of crap," I said to him.

"Are you going to spit in *my* face now?" he asked with a sneer?

"Nope. I'm going to read a poem I wrote."

Brian rolled his eyes.

I returned to my hard little chair, opened my briefcase, and pulled out a folder. I spread the poems flat on the floor, selected one, and held the sheet of paper close to Brian so that he could read along with me. I drew in a deep breath in recognition of that place, and then I read:

### The Good Sumarian

They say the oldest drawings
Of constellations are seals and vases
And game boards, four-thousand B.C.,
So I tried to be a Sumarian
With pad and pencil at my side
As I looked up in the night sky
To point at a place and another
And claim this the tip of a magnolia petal,
Or this the Pelican Twins
Perhaps a cluster of Chinese chrysanthemums?

From star to star I see a hand,
A small hand to catch the moon.
And Venus? The eye of the dolphin.

Surely I must draw what I see tonight in a poem,
A story dating back to seals and vases
As I look up and dream what shape
The patterns of stars from age to age
Will take if I believe the lines are there
To form the figures of my holy fate.

"Brian, what line do you like the most, here?"

"Could you adjust my sock?"

I looked at him. He looked at me. "The right one or the left," I asked.

"The left one."

As I leaned over and adjusted his sock, Brian said, "I like the line 'To form the figures of my holy fate.'"

That afternoon I told Brian about my wife and babies, about the days when I was in high school. Brian told me that he remembered a time when he could walk just like every other child. In first grade he began to fall a lot. In grammar school he needed crutches. In high school the wheelchair. He said that his mother once had beautiful gardens surrounding the house, but she didn't have the time once he became so ill.

I spent two years visiting the Dunn house. I pushed Brian in his chair up and down the street as we discussed Shakespeare, Emily Dickinson, girls, baseball, radios. I liked the boy.

Not too long after Brian died, Mrs. Dunn said to me, "You treated Brian differently than the other teachers did." I was hurt by what she said.

"But, Mrs. Dunn, I didn't treat him differently. I just treated him the way I treat all my students."

"I know, I know. That is what I mean. You didn't make him feel different. How did you know how to find Brian behind that awful disease? People were so afraid of him. They didn't like his spitting. How were you able to treat him like, well, like Brian?"

"I had a brother Oliver. One day my mother wanted to show me how to feed him. She and I were in the kitchen . . . " And I told Mrs. Dunn about what I saw in Oliver's empty eyes as he felt the tip of the spoon touch his lips.

What did Brian feel as I pushed him in his wheelchair? What does a teacher see when a boy needs oxygen? What does a teacher see when children walk into his classroom in September? Does he see a pension, a contract, a way to make a living, a career? What you do for the least of my brothers you do for me.

In twenty-two years I've had, roughly, twenty-two hundred students in my classes, and I liked every one of them. No, I loved every one of them. Difficult students, smart ones, dull ones, pretty ones, ugly ones, fat ones, skinny ones, I loved them all in their humor and anger, conceits and failures, triumphs and laughter.

One afternoon I happened to be speaking with one of the school administrators about Brian and how well he was doing in English. The man looked up from his desk and easily said, "I don't know why we bother. He's going to die anyway."

A friend of mine was a bishop, a great bishop who was asked, in his retirement, if he would be willing to teach a semester course on religion to a class of women in a prestigious college. My friend agreed.

He spent the half-year with the young women, telling them all he know about religion, its history, philosophy, purpose. He had the students write papers and discuss their own points of view. The day before the last class the bishop stood before his students and said, "If you all come to school tomorrow with a flower in your hair, I will give you all an A+ for the semester."

The next day each woman had a fresh daisy clipped in her hair, and every one received an A+. When the school administrators discovered this, someone said, "But what can we do? He's the bishop."

"Why bother. The boy is going to die anyway."

"The rainbow comes and goes, and lovely is the rose," Wordsworth wrote. Lovely is the rose. Lovely is the student.

"Pull up my head, Mr. de Vinck."

# The Lack of Faith

❧

I think I am disillusioned after all. When I was in college in 1969 there was talk of war protests, fighting the establishment, echoes of John Kennedy's call to do something significant in our lives. Crosby, Stills, Nash, and Young created the melodies that floated from campus to campus to a generation softened with the notion that compassion, forgiveness, and freedom offered us a sense of potential for our abilities to be different and to make a difference in this cynical world.

We weren't called baby boomers yet. We were simply young Americans looking at money, war, sex, education, differently from the way our parents and grandparents looked at such things. Perhaps too much reflection when we are young is dangerous, for action without wisdom often carries disappointing consequences. True tragedy comes, though, when people of experience make decisions not based on the aggregate of wisdom but from ego and the moment's convenience.

President Nixon was in the White House. Robert McNamara knew in his heart that Vietnam was a mistake and should have been stopped years and years earlier.

Contempt on both sides of the political aisle for wisdom has so crippled the nation that we have a world today thrashing about on the stock market under a false notion of value, most media outlets are so desperate for a share of the audience's attention that each rape, murder, scandal is a rating's hook that pumps more advertising dollars into a cycle ready to implode if a sudden lack of ugliness stopped the next day's flow of money and curiosity seekers.

By now I would think that the students of George McGovern and the Beatles are in positions of authority and influence. I would think that there would be a significant increase in compassion, innovation, and wisdom in our corporate board rooms and in classrooms across America.

I would think that by now all the cynics and the stodgy naysayers of the establishment in the 1960s and early 1970s would be retired or dead, giving us the opportunity to make significant changes in the way we treat one another. But I look around and everyone calls my generation baby boomers, yuppies, middle America. My generation has taken over. We have a young president in the White House, women fighter pilots, prosecuting attorneys, authors, plumbers, advertising executives, book agents, corporate managers. We from the sixties and seventies have filled the vacant chairs on Wall Street and Main Street. And I look around and what do I see? Certainly not the age of Aquarius.

Most of the books we write and publish are ugly and pessimistic. Most of the movies we create are vapid and gutless. Most of our newspapers define the news instead of reporting it. We create television programs that horrify us. We buy and sell for short-term gain.

Can anyone say that we are in the age of reason or compassion or beauty or confidence or reflection or triumph? Our city and rural schools are in horrible shape; racism is now the unspoken secret; corporate decisions are made more and more in deference to the stockholders and less and less to the men and women on the assembly line who are trying to get their children into sports leagues run by parents who believe that winning is more important than playing ball.

# Faith

When I was a junior in high school I read *The Grapes of Wrath,* and it was from that book that I learned for the first time what the human heart is capable of accomplishing in the face of economic depravity and oppression. No drought, no loss of loved ones, no beating, hunger, or flood was going to stop Ma Joad from believing that people have to go on with compassion and dignity. It was that same compassion and dignity I felt existed in the music, the protests, the turmoil our nation witnessed long ago when I thought long hair and jeans meant that we were going to be a kinder, gentler generation.

Tell me one baby boomer today on a national level who represents my generation's call for wisdom and compassion? Tiger Woods is too young. Mother Teresa was too old. Much of corporate America is squeezing the worker harder and harder. We are printing fewer and fewer books because of their literary merits. We give extraordinary attention to ugliness.

When I look at the faces of today's decision-makers, they all seem to be in their forties and fifties, and I don't recognize them as the same people who believed it was significant to attend Woodstock in the rain and mud simply because there might be a chance that we could change the world into something a bit better than it was before we arrived.

My father is eighty-five years old. He was born the year the Titanic sank, lived through two world wars and the Korean war and the Cuban missile crisis and the Vietnam war. He was a writer, teacher, editor, father, husband. He took me swimming and sailing on a wide lake in Ontario, and it was my father who wrote me a letter when I was in college and said, "Wisdom plays on the surface of the earth in complete freedom of perfect love. We human beings, alas, have spoiled it in part, and much of the spirit of childlike play has been taken away from us; much toil and labor and anguish has been added in its stead. But all spirit of joy, all spirit of spontaneous happiness, has not vanished forever. No longer is it the bread of each day. Yet wisdom does appear as a rare and elusive wonder on those occasions that combine inner peace with some surplus of vital energy left over from the labor of living."

I labor over living the ideals of my lazy generation, which has forgotten what it is like to believe we can strive for joy and happiness, that elusive wonder of a self who acts on what is felt in the heart and not in the stock portfolio.

The face of the world that we in the '60s and '70s so much fought against when we were young turns out to be our own grimace.

# Friends

*I get by with a little help from my friends.*

Paul McCartney

# Teacher as Friend

❧

It was my last year as a teacher, it was June, and my students were coming to their last day of school with thoughts of summer jobs, vacations, and college. I always held a end-of-the-year discussion with my classes as a means to sum up what it was we had done. I wanted to see what they thought of the journey that we took together during the preceding ten months. I wanted to see if they could come up with conclusions about all the books and poems and stories and plays we had read together. What, in the end, does it all mean?

This was the last American literature class I would ever teach. This was my last day as a teacher. We read that year *My Antonia*, *The Great Gatsby*, *The Grapes of Wrath*, *The Glass Menagerie*, *As I Lay Dying*, *To Kill a Mockingbird*, *Death of a Salesman*, Emily Dickinson, Walt Whitman, William Carlos Williams, Robert Frost, Anne Sexton, Mary Oliver, the journals of Madeleine L'Engle and May Sarton.

I asked the students to take out their notebooks. Throughout the year they were asked to collect quotations from the books and poems that they liked. I asked them to write down their observations, their interpretations, their notions about what they read and liked, and then I stepped behind my desk.

"Oh, no," John Meyers groaned. "He's going to do that 'pull-a-poem-out-of-his-magic-briefcase' bit again."

"Shhhhhhhhh," I whispered.

"Mr. de Vinck, you already did this, in the beginning of the year, remember?" a girl laughed.

"Shhhhhhhh," I placed my finger to my lips. And then I handed out one of my poems, the same poem I had used again and again from year to year, from class to class, along the journey I sought when it was my time to seek what was essential in the hearts of young people who sat before me with hope and anticipation, or what ought to be hope and anticipation. You see, teaching is not politics, not issues of the political right or left, not something to be manipulated with dollars and votes. No, hope and anticipation, that is what we "sell" in schools, that is the market, that is the choice.

The only way I knew how to sell hope was to exhibit evidence, and for me the evidence was found in books and plays and poems. For me the dialogue between the children and their teacher is what mattered, and so, as a starting point to end the last day of my teaching career and the last day of the school year, I said, "Okay, let's put our desks into a circle," as I stood before the class:

### Winter

> We take our voices from the dead
> To those who have lingered up ahead
> Where we see them gathering sticks
> For the fuel of a coming winter,
> They who have seen the beginning and the end:
> Steam rising from a foal just born
> And later found frozen in the hedgerow
> Between the new waking and the wet mane
> covered in snow.
>
> Old death sings where cornstalks rattle.
> We know the words but not the melody,
> We cannot distinguish between the flesh

And dew, both to cover what will open:
Earth and bone resolved to wither, one as she
Rolls around the wearing sun, and we who
Close the windows and hope less cold will come
With each new visit of low grief in this familiar
Season.

After the desks were placed in a circle, I gave each student a copy of this poem, and then I asked what connections they might be able to make between what Frost said and what we read throughout the year. The students saw right away what I was after.

"Well," Terry said, "it's true. In the second stanza there it is: 'We hope less cold will come.' Remember how long Gatsby waited to see Daisy again? He spent his whole life making lots of money only to impress her."

"Yeah," John added. "Remember all those parties he gave, and he wasn't even there. He was hoping that Daisy would show up. That was the only reason he gave those parties, to attract her, like a moth to a light. He must have spent a lot of money. He was waiting for a long time for Daisy. He had that hope."

"And what about Jem and Scout in *To Kill a Mockingbird*," Janet reminded us all, as we sat in that circle. "They wanted Boo to come out. They spent all that time watching that strange house, thinking about Boo, that he was a monster or something, and then when Scout figured it all out, she grew up. It took her time, but she got it. She stood on that porch at the end of the book, and she saw what mattered."

"What mattered, Janet?" I asked.

"Well, that Boo saved her life?"

"Yes, but I think there was something more." I asked the class, "What mattered to Scout at the end of the book?"

"Well," Len said, "in the poem you said that death sings. Scout, I mean, isn't it true in a way that death sings if we believe in heaven? Scout died a bit when she discovered Boo was nice. And Boo, he finally came out of the house to save the children. In the end they did meet, they understood each other. Something like that, Mr. de Vinck?"

"Yes, Len, exactly like that. Who else can see a connection between the poem and what we have read this year?"

"I think there is a good line in the poem," Mary offered. "The part where it says 'steam rising from a foal.' It's shocking, a bit, seeing the dead horse. Remember in *As I Lay Dying*, how everyone's life in the book changed when the mother died, and how they tried to bury her the right way? That was a shock to them."

"What does it mean?" I asked the class. "Do shocks keep us sane?"

"I like change," a boy said. "Change helps you look forward to things. Keeps you sane. If life was the same *every* day forever, wouldn't that be terrible?"

"Yeah," another boy laughed. "Look at us. In school for eleven years. We need a change."

"Summer!" Kerry called out to my left. We all laughed.

"But changes can be hurtful too," John added. Jim Burden, in *My Antonia*, his memory of his childhood, didn't that haunt him in a way? Wasn't he sad, thinking that it was over, and he misses what it was like?"

We spoke about May Sarton's loneliness, Willy Loman's need for attention. A girl said that she wants to be a writer, especially after reading Madeleine L'Engle's *Crosswick Journals*. We spoke about how much Mary Oliver likes nature, and how Emily Dickinson seemed to like living alone.

"I remember," said a boy, "how William Carlos Williams suggested that we make our grief visible. Remember in his poem 'Tract' how he was angry that so much is false even in how we bury people? I liked that idea somehow."

# Friends

Toward the end of the period, I asked the students, "What did all these people in the books and poems and plays we've read this year, what did they want ultimately?"

"An 'A' in English?" a boy suggested hopefully.

I walked to the blackboard and made a list of people from some of the books: Willy Loman, J. Gatsby, Laura Wingate, Boo Radley. The class looked at the board, and they looked at me, and then the silence.

"What is it that they all wanted?"

"Well," Terry said, "Willy Loman was lonely, I guess."

"Yeah, so what did he want?"

"Money and fame?" a girl suggested.

"I think he wanted his past back, like Jim Burden," John said. "Just like in *My Antonia*. Willy missed his family, like it used to be."

"You are getting close," I suggested. "What is it that these people wanted in their lives? What do we all want in our lives?"

And so, on the last day of the year, on the last day of my teaching career, a girl raised her hand and simply said, "Love, Mr. de Vinck, all these people wanted love. Willy wanted his sons to love him. He wanted his customers to love him. He wanted his wife to express love, maybe even make love to him in the way he wished, or probably in any way. And Boo Radley. He just wanted the kids to love him. Remember how he stuffed the tree with little gifts, the dolls, the watch. Boo wasn't standing in his house and looking with an evil eye and laughing with an evil laugh. He liked Jem and Scout. Boo laughed with the kids. He wanted to run down the street with them. He wanted to be a part of them. And Gatsby, he wanted Daisy to love him, and May Sarton, all those years of loneliness, and remember how William Carlos Williams said in a poem, 'I'm lonely, lonely, I was born to be lonely.' I think everyone in the things we've read this year wanted to be loved."

"The steam rising from a foal just born?" a boy asked. "Like in the poem?"

"Yes, Jim, just like that. The steam rising," I said. "Where else do you remember images of hope in what we read this year?"

There was silence in the class. I looked around at my last students: John, Terry, Janet, and I saw the faces of all the children who had sat before me for twenty years: youth, hope, arrogance, impatience, humor, ease, boredom, recognition. My students belonged to me when I was a teacher. The calendar revolved around my desk in the summer faces, in the autumn faces, in the winter and spring faces of my students.

"Mr. de Vinck, in *The Grapes of Wrath*, when Rose of Sharon gave her milk. Was there calmness there?" Janet asked. "I wrote in my journal what Steinbeck said, remember the last lines of the book? Remember that sick man in the barn who was starving, and his son came to Ma and begged for help? Remember that Rose of Sharon had just lost her baby, but her breasts were full of milk; and she nursed the man? Is that what you are talking about, Mr. de Vinck? That kind of hope?"

"Yes, Janet, that kind of hope. It's in all the books we've read. It is in all the great books we've read."

"She loved the stranger as she loved herself?"

"Yes."

The bell rang, the students stood up from the circle, and then they walked out of the room one by one.

It was the last period of the day, and the last period of my teaching career. When the room was empty, I stepped out into the hall and listened to the hundreds of students cheering, emptying their lockers, rushing out to the buses. I knew what I was going to do. I walked along hallways that were dull and in need of new wax.

## Friends

I walked among the boys and girls. "Have a good summer, Mr. de Vinck." "See ya, Mr. de Vinck." I was making my way to the front of the building. "Goodbye, Mr. de Vinck."

"Goodbye," I said to many students. "Have a good summer." I walked and walked, weaving in and out among the children as they too walked toward the front of the school. Then I stopped and stood before the large glass windows and looked out at the thirty or forty yellow buses. Soon they were filled. Boys and girls waved out the windows to their friends, or sat in their seats and laughed. I stood there and watched the buses pull out one by one, and I prayed that the hope of the world would last for my students somehow as they made their way through the calm of winter.

# My Friend May Sarton

Writers meet writers at conferences, in the halls of publishing houses, through letters, through mutual friends, and why not? Dairy farmers meet other dairy farmers over their shared interest in milk. Fashion designers tip their hats to each other in European restaurants. Carpenters meet to discuss the price of lumber.

While writers do not work with milk, cloth, or wood, the primary ingredients of our survival (food, clothing, and shelter), they do manipulate material of a different sort, ideas, and for a different sort of survival, "green-bean" survival.

Many years ago I was introduced, by a mutual friend, to the poet, novelist, and journal writer May Sarton. From the very beginning May and I were fast friends. She invited me to visit her in York, Maine, her last home, which had for its front yard a patio, stone wall, garden, another stone wall, tall weeds, rocks, the rush of water, and finally, the Atlantic Ocean.

I think of May today for I received, in the mail, a letter from a woman in Virginia. "I am writing to you because when I was recently reading one of May Sarton's books, she mentioned that you had stopped by for a visit at her home in Maine. She is one of my favorite women authors, and it makes me sad to think there will be no more of her wonderful journals. Have you written a remembrance of her?"

# Friends

I had not written such a thing, for May is still alive and rich in my life. Of course there are no more letters in my mailbox postmarked York, Maine. There are no more yearly visits, but her books are on my shelf beside my desk where I write, her picture sits in a small, brown frame, an empty bottle of wine sits on my desk with dried wheat sprouting from the neck.

I do not have to discuss milk and clothes and lumber with May in order to be with her. All I have to do is open her *Journal of Solitude*, and we are together again. Writers deal with the commodity of the soul. The poet Walt Whitman understood this expanding universe of human will and con-sciousness, something that holds all people together beyond death. He speculated that perhaps we are all, combined, the living God. At least Whitman rang the gong of his existence, and the sounds still reverberate across the consciousness of all serious writers in America today.

During one of my visits May asked me if I knew anything about smoke alarms. She explained that the one at the top of the stairs had been emitting a periodic, loud beep for days, and it had been causing her great distress. I drove out to a local hardware store, returned, climbed a small ladder, opened the casing to the smoke detector, and replaced the battery.

May cooked the first fresh lobster I had ever eaten. She asked me to open the bottle of wine. In the kitchen, as she snapped the green beans, she said, "I love the sound of beans snapping." After dinner she asked me to sit beside her in her living room and read aloud some of my work.

May wrote, in one of her spring letters, "I have planted rows and rows of annuals [seeds], ever hopeful." Although May spent many years alone, she clearly knew the difference between loneliness and solitude. She chose solitude, which leads to a contemplative life, and vigorously and triumphantly fought loneliness as she leaned over the open spring earth and was always hopeful.

There is a secret all true writers know, and that is the pull between the merriment of writing and the anguish of digging deep within oneself in order to detect bits of that universal soul.

A surgeon once said to me that there comes, over time, an intuition about his craft, a feeling in the hands that burns beyond knowledge and experience, a sense for a pressure, or tear, or combination of blood and distress that signals a diagnosis juxtaposed with the use of a scalpel and sutures that is difficult to describe, except to another surgeon.

One reason people who struggle with similar vocations like to get together is to discuss the secrets of their trade and to encourage each other to go on, to continue, for the rewards are great in the coming spring of seeds and green beans. May often gave me such encouragement. She was forty years older than I was, and willing to give me what was given to her, that push, that support, that sound of a spiritual survival, the sound of beans snapping.

"I haven't read the Macleish biography," May wrote in midsummer, "but am so happy to hear that he encouraged you when you were starting out. Such an incredibly generous man. He was very kind to me when I was a lowly instructor at Harvard and he was Professor of Poetry, but do not envy him. . . . Paris was not that good in the very long run for American artists, intoxicating, yes, but I think maybe your basement room is richer ground."

I struggle daily with the intoxication of being a writer and the sounds of the children plopping their books on the kitchen table as they return home from school, but May said to me again and again, not Paris, but Roe and my children and my intimate friends, there I will find the heart of milk, cloth, and wood for my own poems, novels, and essays.

May Sarton wrote on her desk in the third floor of her house. She could look up and see the ocean, or find her cat

## *Friends*

Tammas curled up in an unexpected place in her room. She read the journals of Julian Green in the evening, wrote, planted seeds in the ground of New England and in my own heart and in the hearts of thousands of people who read her work.

Writers meet writers every day. Read her journals, and you will taste the fresh lobster, feel the smooth fur of Tammas under your hands; you will hear the sounds of beans snapping, ever hopeful.

# The Friendship of a Stranger

❦

We are award crazy. We give out prizes for best movies, best books, best television programs, best commercials, best print advertisements, best athletes, best teams, best cows, best spellers.

We distribute millions of diplomas, medals, ribbons, certificates of achievement. There is a thriving store in my town that mass produces trophies for bowling leagues, business achievements, Father's Day. We give awards for best writers, best airlines, best schools. Everywhere we look in our society, we find someone seeking an award or bestowing an award.

We praise and praise and praise, and yet I do not think the awards system we have created is worth very much to either the giver or the receiver of such accolades.

I recently flew to Chicago, originating from Newark, New Jersey. I hadn't taken a trip in several months and was delighted to see the new monorail in service at the airport. I parked my car, took the escalator up to the top platform. The station had beautiful metal handrails, a simple and strong design. The monorail was comfortable and convenient.

Once inside the airport, a Continental customer-service agent helped me with my ticket, assured me that I would not miss my plane. Just before I sat in my seat of the Boeing 737, a flight attendant helped me adjust my luggage in the overhead compartment. The music of Aaron Copland played quietly in the background.

During the flight we were given a delicious turkey sandwich, a cold can of Coca-Cola, a small Baby Ruth candy bar. I read the *Wall Street Journal* on my way to Chicago; relaxed in my Lee jeans.

If you walk into a Continental terminal you cannot help but see banners, stickers, and notices that the airline won an award from J. D. Power as the best airline for customer satisfaction for long distance service. Continental is obviously proud of this award, as it ought to be, and J. D. Power ought to be proud of the respect that is bestowed upon it.

As I entered the 737, I saw a J. D. Power award sticker glued right onto the plane. When we landed and pulled up to the terminal, after we, the passengers, were allowed to unbuckle our seat belts and retrieve our luggage from the overhead compartments, we all began slowly to walk single file out of the plane. The airline pilot stood outside the cockpit and said goodbye to each person. I stopped just for a moment and said, "That was wonderful."

The pilot turned his head a bit.

"You flew this extraordinary airplane with all of us on board. It is an amazing thing that you did, and I just wanted to say thank you."

The pilot said in his deep, wonderful, pilot voice, "Well, thank you very much. Have a good day." And then he extended his hand. I am sure the award from J. D. Power meant a great deal to the entire corporation of Continental, and I am sure that my handshake meant a great deal to the airline pilot.

I happen to know a man who pops rivets into the Boeing 737 aircraft. I asked Brian what it is like working in the assembly plant on such an airplane. "The design, the safety, the size. It is amazing that something this big and this sophisticated flies. I am proud to be a part of it." I said to Brian that each time I step into a jet liner, I look at a bolt or a rivet and think, "Perhaps Brian stood right here, building this plane."

I wish I could shake the hands of the people who designed the Boeing 737-300. I told Brian that I will soon be flying to Chicago, and I thanked him for his work and for being my friend.

On the wrapper of the Baby Ruth candy bar there is an 800 number to call for questions or comments. I wanted to make a comment, so I called. I explained that I am a freelance writer, and I was working on a little article about awards, and how much I'd like to shake the hand of the person who left home early to arrive at work on time, that person who hung up his or her coat, greeted friends, walked down to the assembly floor and began his or her day checking the quality of the chocolate mix, or making sure the peanuts were evenly distributed.

The woman at the corporate headquarters in California could not have been nicer. She explained that there was a celebration at the Baby Ruth plant where they created a 75 pound candy bar in celebration of the seventy-fifth anniversary of the existence of Baby Ruth.

I explained to the customer service department that each Friday evening when I was a boy, my father and mother came home from the weekly food shopping and gave me a Baby Ruth candy bar. I saved it until I was in bed with my book, and read three pages, then took a bite of my candy, read another three pages, and took another bite. I remember doing this while I was reading *Treasure Island*.

I said to the woman, "Could you thank someone at the candy factory for me?"

"I will," the woman answered. There was a pause, and then she added earnestly, "You know, I really will. Thank you, really. Thank you."

"That's the point," I said. "And thank you!"

# Friends

"By the way," the woman in the candy headquarters said, "I loved *Treasure Island* too."

The anthropologist Loren Eisely wrote about the blessed mystery of opening an ancient tomb, or brushing away the dust around a newly discovered clay pot someone made over three thousand years ago. Can you imagine seeing the thumbprint of another human being pressed into the side of a bowl made thousands of years ago?

In a pocket of my Lee jeans I found a small slip of paper: "Inspected by #36." How much I would like to thank inspector #36 for my comfortable pants. How much I would like to shake the hand of the person who made these jeans. Like the ancient thumbprint, there is evidence that my clothes were made by a human being, someone out there with a family, with a work schedule, someone who might like a handshake from someone in New Jersey.

At the end of my first ride on the monorail at Newark Airport, I stepped up to the front of the small train because I wanted to thank the operator for a wonderful ride. I looked inside the first car, and then I realized that there was no conductor. The train is automated, computerized, flawless, quiet, smooth, comfortable. I'd like to congratulate the design team that created this machine.

After my talk in Chicago, three people stepped up to the podium: a man and two women. One of the women quickly said, "We've been friends for years, the three of us. We go on vacations with our families. Last summer I found your book. We stayed up for two nights reading your little essays aloud. We laughed. We cried. We just wanted to tell you what your writing has meant to us," and then all three reached out their hands at once and the four of us, like in a basketball huddle, held hands together in a small circle.

Just like that. I want to stand in a circle with the people from Baby Ruth, from Lee jeans, from Continental Airlines, from Newark Airport, from Boeing, and hold hands together, one big handshake, a nice award for us all, it seems to me, the circle complete: a product made and a product delivered, and in-between a human response, a direct link between producer and consumer, friends perhaps.

# The Luck of a Brother-in-law
## as a Friend

❧

We were in Peter's basement, my eleven-year old son Michael and I. Peter is my brother-in-law, an artist, engineer, mechanic, tennis player, carpenter, welder, actor, father, husband, landscaper, helicopter pilot, scuba diver. He was demonstrating his latest hobby: model trains.

He set up tracks, switches, lights, trees, on a wide piece of plywood, and he let Michael control the train with the blue transformer. The small engine click-clacked around and around the pattern of loops and curves. "Hey," Michael said with glee, "it even goes backward."

We were nearly finished with our Saturday afternoon visit when Peter reached up to the top of a gray, metal shelf and asked, "Michael? Would you be interested in having your own set of trains?"

Would Captain Nemo be interested in a submarine? Would Wilbur and Orville be interested in an airplane? Would Richard II be interested in a horse?

Michael and I drove home that night with the whole Santa Fe Railroad Company packed in a yellow box sitting on the back seat of the car. Peter had bought the set a few months earlier at a garage sale for thirty-five dollars.

I knew what was coming. I've spent my life with the same dread. I can hear my sister asking me to fix the chain on her bike. "It just fell off." I can hear my father asking me to start the lawn mower for the first time in the spring. I can hear my son asking, "Dad? Can we build a tree fort?"

I pinched my finger in the bicycle chain and walked it to the bike shop, those many years ago when I was a boy. I pulled and pulled on the rope to the lawn mower until my father stepped out from the house, yanked out the spark plug, rubbed the tip with a bit of sandpaper, and replaced the plug. "Give it a pull," he said. I pulled, and the machine roared to a new summer life.

I did build a tree fort with Michael, but the Swiss Family Robinson, if they were my relatives, would have immediately put me up for adoption if they saw what I managed to produce.

To say that I am not very clever with my hands is like saying a fish is not very good at surgery.

My wife asked me if I would put a dimmer switch in the dining room, so I bought the switch, carried my pliers and screwdriver up from the basement, unscrewed the switch plate from the wall . . . and then I imagined the cobra, the fangs, the poison, the strike, the beast that would lunge out from the exposed wires and, in one quick flash of venom and sparks, kill me.

I screwed the switch plate back onto the wall, and then I played Monopoly with the children.

I've had some successes in my life. I own a 1929 Model A Ford, and one afternoon, as I was driving the car with my two sons, the car hit a bump, and suddenly stopped. I turned the key. Nothing happened. I was able to connect, in my mind, the notion that if there wasn't any power, there might be something wrong with the battery. I picked up the floor mat, unclipped the flat piece of wood that covered the battery, and there I saw one of the cables had been knocked off the battery stem.

Well, I felt like a genius when I pushed the cable back onto the battery terminal and, with a single turn of the key, the Model A started immediately. That was the same afternoon I almost rammed into a car ahead of me because I didn't realize my brakes were so precariously worn and lined with grease and oil.

A local mechanic, who spent thirty years repairing Ford Model A's, replaced my brakes. When I told him my battery cable story, mechanic to mechanic, he just looked up at me from under the car and smiled.

"Dad? Can you help me with the trains?" Michael called the next day from our basement. I knew it.

Five years ago John, my other brother-in-law (college professor, engineer, electrician, carpenter, musician, etc.) helped me finish the basement. Actually, he did the planning, the measuring, the cutting, and I, when John pointed, took nails and hammered.

"Dad? I can't get this train to work," Michael said as he looked up at me from the set of tracks connected in a circle. "I don't know where the transformer goes. We need wire, and there isn't an instruction book."

It is a good thing that I was not Thomas Edison's father. "Dad, I just can't seem to find the right filament to make this light bulb glow for an extended period of time."

"Well, Tom, it's not important. Why don't you put all that stuff away for now and go do your homework and become a lawyer or something."

"Uncle Peter said that he got this set to work. Can you help me?"

"Let me see what I can do." I reached for my pliers and screwdriver, found some wire, attached one wire to the transformer and then to the track, then I did the same with a second wire. "See how we screw the wire in here, and here?" I showed Michael with the tip of the screwdriver.

"Can I do that?" he asked.

"Sure."

Michael turned the screw; it slowly tightened against the wire. He repeated the operation with the second wire. We were all set. I plugged in the transformer. Michael placed the green engine on the tracks, making sure that the wheels were properly adjusted, and then he flipped the switch. Nothing.

"I think you should call Uncle Peter," Michael suggested.

"I know what I'm doing!" I snapped. I fiddled with the wire. I plugged a lamp into the socket to make sure we were getting an electric current. We were. I squeezed the tracks together. Switched transformers twice. Switched engines twice. Crossed wires, and I tried and I tried, but no matter what I did, nothing. Where was Thomas Edison? Captain Nemo? The Wright Brothers?

That night, Michael reminded me, "Dad, you don't have to get so mad about the train set." It was too difficult to explain how disappointed I was for him. It was too difficult to explain how frustrated I felt at my own inability to launch a rocket to the moon, or get an eight-inch train engine to make a few laps around a set of miniature tracks, and I couldn't tell him about my own failures as a father.

A few days later, Peter did arrive, feeling upset about my frustration, knowing that the train didn't work, and anxious to bring the set alive for Michael.

We followed Peter to the basement as he pulled his Swiss Army Knife from his right pocket. He jiggled wires, pushed the engine along the tracks a few times, then he simply picked up the track that was attached to the transformer and pointed with the tip of his knife. "See that? No connection."

Peter unscrewed the wire from the track, found another track with the same little screws, the track for the transformer, used his pocket knife, screwed in the wires, plugged in the transformer. Wheels spun. Lights glowed. The little engine I thought could not, could, and did spin around and around the tracks. It did lose power in various places, until Peter wiped all the tracks with a light coating of oil, then the train loped around the basement as if it were on skates.

"How good are you with dimmer switches?" I asked.

When my father was a young man growing up in Europe, he built sailboats and sailed on the Atlantic Ocean and on wide lakes in Belgium. He often said proudly, "I made those boats without a single power tool."

I can build novels, create essays, construct sentences, but if you ask me to adjust the lens of the Hubble telescope, or to wire a telephone in a bedroom, or to fix the toaster, I'll call Uncle Peter.

# Friendship with a Stubborn Grandfather

❧

It is easy to forget how much we love one another, especially when we are angry. I learned this painful lesson when I was twelve years old during a summer morning during those long-ago days when my grandparents came to visit from Belgium.

My grandfather, whom we called Bon Papa (good father), was a general in the Belgian army, and my grandmother, whom we called Baba (I don't know why) was, well a grandmother: filled with generosity, patience, and ice-cream treats. My grandfather was also filled with generosity and ice-cream treats, but he had little patience, especially with a grandson who could, at times, be disrespectful.

As I walked by the refrigerator one day in July, Bon Papa barked an order.

"Boy! Get me a beer out of the refrigerator!"

I looked as his hair as he leaned over his plate of food.

"No!" I answered.

"Boy! I said get me a beer out of the refrigerator!" Bon Papa leaned forward in his chair. My sister stopped slurping her soup and looked up at me. My grandmother sat still.

"You can get it yourself. You're not crippled." I looked blindly in Bon Papa's direction, then I walked out of the kitchen.

# Friends

My grandfather *was* crippled. In the First World War, during heavy fighting in the flat farmlands of central Europe, my grandfather was shot in the upper portion of his left arm. When he was on the operating table at the military hospital, he begged the doctor not to cut off his arm. Just before Bon Papa was given the anesthesia, he whispered, "Please don't cut off my arm."

The doctors at that time didn't know anything about microsurgery. All they knew was that they had a soldier with a hole in his left arm as big as a baseball.

When Bon Papa woke up in the recovery room, he picked up his right hand and began feeling his left shoulder down, down, down to his elbow. The doctors did not cut off his arm, which was just about all they could do for my grandfather. Ever since that day, Bon Papa's left arm was a useless appendage, like a broken wing. He couldn't lift or grasp anything with his left hand. In all the pictures of my grandfather he is holding his left arm behind his back.

*However*, Bon Papa had two perfectly good legs, and a perfectly good right hand. He had the ability to stand up from his kitchen chair, walk four feet, open the refrigerator, fish around deep inside the cold box, grab a beer, and return to his seat. I was confident I had done the right thing. A kid has to stand up for what he believes in, even at the risk of breaking ranks.

After I announced my brave "no," I stepped out of the kitchen and casually walked through the dining room on my way to the television in the living room.

I happened to glance behind me, and there I saw a madman in a white shirt and khaki pants flailing his right hand over his head. He was trailing gray smoke behind him.

I was startled to see that Bon Papa's face had turned red. But not a piece of his white hair fell out of place even though he nearly flew across the room as he tried to grab hold of me. "Monster!"

For my own protection, I ran around the dining-room table. *He* began to run around the table. Each time I increased my speed, he too ran faster and faster. On our third trip around the table, we were both running hard.

"Come here! I order you!" His left arm flapped against his side.

I saw that his anger was not going to subside quickly, so I ran out the dining room and into the foyer. I intended to run upstairs and into my room and forget the whole thing.

"Where do you think you are going?" My grandfather kept chasing me. "Come here immediately!"

I turned quickly to the right and began running up the stairs. When I reached the first landing, I stopped, turned, and waited for Bon Papa to reach the bottom of the stairs.

"Are you going to listen to me, boy?" he screamed.

I leaned forward a bit, stood at a rigid attention, snapped my grandfather a sharp salute, and answered down to him with a great flourish, "Yes sir, General!"

He looked as if he had been shot in the *right* arm. He staggered back for a brief second, then Bon Papa grabbed the banister with his good hand and began pulling himself up the stairs with great speed. His left arm flapped again and again against his side.

I zoomed up the rest of the stairs and ran down the long, narrow hall past my bedroom. I turned around at the end of the hall and, once again, waited.

When Bon Papa finally reached the top of the stairs, I regained my confidence. He stood at the opposite end of the hallway and raised his good arm above his head.

"When I catch you, I am going to beat you until de Gaulle rises from the dead, boy! Monster!"

Behind my grandfather was a large window with bright sunlight shooting into the hall. Because he was standing in front of the window, all I could see was his dark silhouette and his arm waving back and forth above his head.

"I'm going to beat you!"

"Qui, mon general!" I barked in my mock French accent.
He and all of Europe charged down the hall for what seemed
to be the final assault. I turned to my right, then quickly to the
right once again, and then I ran down the back stairs.

In the house where I grew up there was the wide front
staircase with the fancy carpet and the oak banister, and there
was the back stairs: narrow, dark, twisting. Because there was
no banister to support him, Bon Papa never used those stairs.
I knew that.

I jumped down three steps at a time. At the bottom of the
stairs I leaned against the closed door and ended up right back
where the battle had begun: in the kitchen. My sister was still
sitting before her bowl of soup. Baba stood in the middle of
the kitchen weeping. I walked up to my grandmother and tried
to comfort her.

"Oh, Christopher, why are you doing this?" she pleaded.
Whenever my grandmother spoke with someone, she had the
habit of grabbing onto his or her arm. Perhaps that is why
many people walked away from her when she began to
speak.

"Christopher! Won't you make up with your grandfather?"
Baba said as she clamped her hand tightly onto my right arm;
meanwhile we all could hear Thump! Thump! Thump! Bon
Papa was running back through the upstairs hallway. "Your
mother will be disappointed with you when she comes home
from the shopping."

That is when I felt as if *I* had been shot.

Thump! Thump! Thump! Bon Papa was making his way
down the front stairs.

"Christopher! Please make up with your grandfather!"

Thump! Thump! Thump! Bon Papa crashed through the
dining room. Then, wham, he broke through the last line of
defense and charged into the kitchen, reaching for my neck.

I broke free from my grandmother. My sister took a sip of
soup from her spoon, and Bon Papa stumbled over the
kitchen chair. I ran backward, hit the back door, turned the
handle, ran across the porch, leaped down the stairs, ran past
my grandfather's rose garden, and then I disappeared into the
dark woods, where I stopped and waited.

Bon Papa exploded onto the porch and began pacing back
and forth. If he had had a Bazooka, he would have used it on
me, on the woods, on the entire battlefield just to flush me
out, or to finish me off.

I knew he couldn't see me in the woods, and I knew he
wouldn't chase after me over the rough terrain.

"Just you wait, boy!" he screamed out across the wide
distance between us. "Just you wait, monster! We aren't
finished! You'll have to come in for dinner eventually!" He
turned, stepped into the house, grabbed the door, and yanked
it shut. Boom! Slam! Bang!

Of course he was right. I couldn't have stayed in the woods
forever, unless I became the next Robin Hood. The idea of
running away did cross my mind, except I didn't want to leave
my sister behind.

I spent the rest of the afternoon searching for salamanders
(I found none), and climbing trees (I couldn't see the city).
Finally I did return to the house for dinner.

And so the cold war began. I sat down at the supper table
with my sister to my left, and with my grandmother to my
right. My grandfather sat on the other side of the table as he
glared at me. After my father said grace, we began passing the
food from person to person. It didn't matter that the small
bowl of gravy sat just to the right of my plate. Bon Papa said
politely to my *sister,* "Would you please pass the gravy?"

Fine, I thought. I too can play the game. I asked Baba if she
would you please pass the beans, which were near my grandfather.

## Friends

After dinner, Bon Papa stood up from the table, walked
past my chair, giving it a quick kick, then he walked outside to
tend to his roses.

My mother said, "Christopher, stop this. Make up with your
grandfather and be done with this nonsense."

"I'm not making up to him. He can make up to me."

A few days later, I ran out of the living room and up the
front stairs. I wasn't paying much attention, for if I had I would
have noticed that Bon Papa was already halfway down the
stairs by the time I was halfway up. I wasn't about to back
down, and he wasn't about to back up, so we slowly passed
each other on the stairs. As I walked to his right, he quickly
slapped the back of my head. I ran up the stairs. He won a
little battle, but not the war.

As the summer progressed, my grandfather and I continued
to ignore each other. One night, as I was just about to fall
asleep, my bedroom door slowly opened. I pretended to be
sleeping. I left my eyes open just enough for me to see how
fast a Bazooka could kill a kid.

Slowly . . . slowly . . . the door opened wider and wider.
The door frame filled completely with the shape of a person.
Closer . . . closer the person slowly approached my bed.

I was about to scream, but then the figure leaned over my
bed and whispered "Here. Make up with your grandfather."

My grandmother, in her rumpled Chinese bathrobe, extended a ten-dollar bill in my direction.

I looked at my grandmother's pleading eyes. Her teeth were
soaking in a glass on the bathroom sink. Her wig sat on a
Styrofoam head on her bedroom dresser. "Make up with your
grandfather."

"No!" I said.

Baba turned and walked out of my room, and I slept.

It was the last week of October, and my grandparents
walked down the stairs in their traveling clothes. My older

brother and my father carried the suitcases to the car. Baba and Bon Papa were going back to Belgium.

My grandmother kissed my sisters as she wept. She kissed my brothers and me, then she walked out of the house, down the front steps, and into the car.

Then my grandfather hugged my two sisters, shook my brothers' hands. He ignored me. He turned and began walking out the front door. I remember the back of his neatly cut white hair touching the collar of his dark coat. That is when I called out, "I'm sorry."

"Now's a nice time to say that, Chris," my mother scolded.

"I'm sorry, Bon Papa," I said.

My grandfather didn't turn around, didn't respond. He just walked out the front door, walked down the front steps, and made his way into the waiting car. My father drove out the driveway, honking the horn once.

I ran out of the house, and down to the side lawn where I watched my father's white station wagon disappear behind some bushes, reappear, disappear behind the neighbor's house, and reappear. And then the car continued down the street; my grandparents were on their way to the airport. I never saw my grandfather again. A few months later we received a telegram. My grandfather had died in his sleep.

Whenever I think of my grandfather, I try to rearrange the events of my past so that he is there beside me with an open embrace as he steps out of the house for the last time.

My grandfather gave me a lion puppet one summer, took me to the Bronx Zoo and asked if I wanted to ride the elephant. He brought me many times to the ice-cream parlor where he bought me a double-scoop dish of ice cream. There was always the option: a single scoop or a double scoop. He always ordered the double scoop. In one of my visions of heaven I am riding a large, gray elephant as my grandfather stands beyond the fence, waving.

# The Goodwill of America

෴

I was sitting here in the room where I write working on my next book when the brown UPS truck pulled up before the house. "Roe ordered another bedspread," I thought to myself. I opened the door for the delivery man as he carried this large box toward me.

I signed the release form, thanked the driver, and set the package down in the living room. I was anxious to finish a chapter on the computer, so I didn't open the box right away, but I did notice that my name, not my wife's, was printed on the box label.

After working for another hour, I returned to the mysterious parcel sitting on the blue carpet. When I pulled opened the brown flaps and saw all the bubble-wrap, I was even more curious and puzzled. Then, wham! What a delightful surprise: a huge basket of cookies, brownies, candies, cashews, crackers, gum, cakes.

An executive from one of the greatest cookie corporations in the country read my book *The Power of the Powerless* and felt that the story of Oliver, my blind, disabled, mute brother who had no intellect and was fed, bathed, and loved by my mother and father for thirty-two years, had a simple lesson that corporate America seems to be losing, so this man sent my family and me this large container of delicious, splendid American products that are being developed and manufactured, in his opinion, in an environment of distrust, competition, fear, and heartbreak.

"I have been through fourteen separate *downsizings,* including the latest and most painful gutting of the work force, which we euphemistically termed 'a major transformation,' the man wrote to me in a letter attached to a checkered ribbon tied to the basket. "Transformation! This word used to suggest a metamorphosis to something greater, better, or higher. But for most of us in the corporate world, it stands for the most significant shedding of talent, knowledge, and spirit ever witnessed. Your book reminded me of what is truly important."

I read this man's letter and remembered how much my brother loved this company's pudding. (Oliver could not even chew.)

I know the burdens and struggles of maintaining a sense for what is important in this very confused, tempting, hard, violent, profit-seeking world. I, like this man, sometimes feel as if I have failed my family, my writing, myself . . . and these doubts are, I know, the price we have to pay for being reflective people. A contemplative life is perhaps the most difficult life to live for we are, then, always at odds with what could be and what is.

"My company's *transformation* has turned colleagues into competitors and effectively destroyed the interdependency and trust so vital to the success of any organization." This career company man has not lost his sense of reflection, and what he wrote in his letter is not only distressing to hear but confirms my suspicions.

There seems to be a false value being placed on the market. I think Alan Greenspan is right, though he would not be talking about the value of the human heart, but the value of false hype on the worth of a product, but I believe it comes down to the same thing: the bottom line in our economy, if dependent too much on profit, will stretch people to a point where they can no longer recognize who they are and why they are working.

I think we are already seeing this attitude spilling over into the areas of mental disabilities, old age, and welfare reform. In other words, the weakest among us are not being valued, and unless we tend to the weak in our country, all else will crumble, and that includes the work force, which sees itself more and more in a position of weakness.

Where is the America that *saved* Europe in 1946? Where is the politician who speaks from the heart? Where is the company that is balancing the human needs of the worker and the buyer with the need for profit?

I do believe that many corporations in our country are spinning out of control a bit, losing sight of what really matters. Yes, profit is important in our society. It is too bad, in a way, that so much of our world depends on growth. Each year companies not only have to show a profit, but they insist on showing growth and an increase on last year's gains. Well, that is good, but it has to end somewhere, doesn't it? Or reach a point where it has to stabilize?

I think of many products on the shelf. Yogurt, for example. The pots are getting smaller and smaller, and the prices are increasing. How small will the pot of yogurt get and how much are people willing to pay for it? That seems to be the balancing act. Yogurt is such a wonderful food but it is, in my mind, cheapened by the rising cost and the decreasing size.

The automobile corporations tried to do the same thing: build cheaper cars and charge more money, and that created horrible cars and opened the door to quality cars from Japan.

I do think we need, in this country, a renewal of spirit, a sense that we are going to work for a wonderful reason beyond salary and profit. The basket of delicious foods that

arrived on my door step is simply wonderful. Do the workers
at the cookie plant go to work each morning with the idea that
they are making something wonderful, or do they simply drive
to work, do a job, collect a paycheck, and drive home? I think
many people are just doing a job. Those cookies and cakes are
so wonderful. Is there pride in making those things?

I think much of the problem in our country comes from the
lost sense of community within the corporations and their lost
response to the community beyond their parking lots.

Long ago we knew who baked our bread, who made the
horseshoes, who the doctor was, who the farmer was. Today
there is this huge wall that divides those who make the goods
and those who buys the goods. I cannot tell you how often I
wish I could thank someone in person for the delicious orange
I have as a snack in the afternoon. (When my mother was a
child in Belgium, an orange was a rare, rare treat that she only
had, perhaps, at Christmas.)

We take oranges for granted. We take everything for
granted, every product, everything we eat, everything we buy,
everything we create. We have such an extraordinary system in
this country . . . our food supply . . . how safe it is! How good
the food is! How wonderfully wrapped it all is. And we lose
sight of all that. People who make the product are just doing a
job. People who manage the creation of the product are just
trying to make bigger profits. I think bigger profits will come
from the companies that (1) return to the awe of the product
that they are making, and (2) create a sense of community and
purpose in the lives of people who work for them.

I'll tell you a little story. A few years ago I was driving home
with my children and saw, up ahead, the cookie factory where
many of those products that found their way to my doorstep
were made.

I thought to myself, "I wonder if they give tours of the
plant," so I drove into the parking lot, and the children and I

walked into a reception area. We were greeted by a very nice man who said that, no, the plant doesn't give tours. Then he looked at the children and said, with a wonderful smile, "Just wait a second." He disappeared behind a door as the children and I saw two women walk through the area where we were waiting. They were dressed in green protective suits of some sort, and hats of some sort. Obviously they were working in the plant. The children were so intrigued with these women. They thought it was so neat that they were dressed like that. Then the man returned and gave each child an individual box of cookies. The children were thrilled to have those small boxes they knew so well, and the man apologized for not having a tour. But I will tell you this: the children thought that behind those doors was a Willy Wonka super fantastic cookie factory. If I were the head of this company, I'd organize tours of every plant and hire a fellow who looks like that wonderful man we met and make him the guide.

People in television make so much money because they are watched by such a large audience. Airline pilots are watched by so many people. Doctors are observed by so many people. But men and women working in a plant of some sort, who watches them? Who sees what they do? A supervisor? I think too many people today feel that what they are doing isn't important and the only thing that keeps them going is the paycheck.

Remember that recent commercial about the automobile company showing how the workers on the assembly plant have the power to stop the line, and how tourists come into the plant and watch what they are doing? That is really a wonderful idea. I wonder if people in the food corporations know how much fun it is to open a can of cashews and smell the salt and nuts, to dig into the can, to take that first mouthful, especially when no one is home and I can eat the whole can if I like?

I am intrigued with people and with what they do. I am so often compelled to call my sister or brother, or my mother and father, just to thank them for something they did the week before: sending a card to the children, inviting us to dinner, something. My brother-in-law gave me a lawnmower five or six years ago. I still thank him for that gift.

Coming from a house where my powerless brother was on his back in his bed with no intellect for thirty-two years, I learned to be grateful, and that deep sense of gratitude never has left me. I wish I could call up the people who packed my can of cashews and thank them for that delicious treat. As an author, people write me all the time, or call on the phone, or invite me to speak. Who writes those two women in their funny, wonderful, green plant-clothes? Who calls that man who gave my children those cookies?

I know that in the past corporations and their workers became involved in community projects, and that made a huge difference in how people looked at each other in the hallways during the work day. Organizations like Special Olympics have done this for sure. I think a company that nurtures its community with jobs, opportunities, and of course makes great cookies, will be the company that will thrive in the next thousand years.

The culture of corporate America needs to return significant artifacts to the center of what they do: quality products that are developed and manufactured out of a sense of profit *and* goodwill, goodwill that is extended to those who develop, create, and consume the product. Profit without goodwill cannot deliver a promise of corporate growth.

The man who wrote me the letter said, "The simple truth is that corporate America has broken its moorings with virtue and is adrift in a sea of confusion, distrust, and egos. We've lost our vision and with it our heart and passion. No heart . . . no life . . . no growth."

# Husband as Best Friend

❧

$A$s I stood in the hospital recovery room when my first son was born, I was genuinely surprised at what my wife and I had produced: a baby, a boy, a son, a future, a strong wail, a wet bottom.

Although I was prepared for the event, attended the birthing classes, watched Roe's womb expand over the nine moths, nothing could prepare me for the feeling that I had when David was born, as if Roe and I had stumbled across something wonderful. This feeling of discovery returned when Karen and Michael were born.

We go through our lives, our regular days, not expecting much to happen, but then little or big surprises leap up at us suddenly and make us stop and wonder, or laugh, or cry.

I like so much waking in the morning of a winter's day and seeing out the window a new landscape of snow that accumulated during the night. It is best when I didn't read the newspapers or watch the evening forecast, and the snow is a complete surprise.

I am often equally delighted when I rummage through my bookshelf in search of something to read. I return to books I read long ago and have forgotten: a biography of Walt Whitman, a novel by Thomas Hardy, a collection of essays by Loren Eiseley. I click on the lamp beside the shelf, run my hand along the spines of books that stand waiting side by side, like patient children, and then I decide and pull out Robert Frost or Flannery O'Connor or T. S. Eliot. I sit on the green chair under the lamp and open the book.

Often, yes, I find a poem that I remember, or a sentence, and I slip back in a novel or play or dream to a place I lived when I read the book long ago, and often there is something more, something unexpected, that opens before me as the pages part between the book's covers.

I will find a picture my seventeen-year-old son drew when he was five: a horse eating flowers. I will find a poem my daughter wrote ten years ago, or a photograph of Michael on a swing, or pressed flowers from a forgotten spring.

I use my books as a filing system. Well, I have no right to call it a system. If it is Father's Day, and I happen to be reading the diary of Julian Green, I will place the card into the book and use it as a book marker and discover the card five years later and regain the initial delight at receiving the card in the first place.

My notion of retiring in my old age includes sitting on the couch, thumbing through all the photo albums and rereading all the books on my shelf and finding old cards, poems, stories, and pictures created by my children, and then I can die.

Each day we have a new chance for serendipity, a new potential for surprises. The phone rings, and I am suddenly invited to meet the pope in Rome to give him one of my books. The doorbell rings and a student I had twenty years ago appears just to say hello. The mail truck rolls up to the front of the house, and I receive a letter from a woman living in Ohio.

> When I wrote in my previous letter about my husband, Bob, dying after seven years of coping with lym- phoma, I didn't go into detail. But his many tests previous to diagnosis had us waiting for two weeks

# *Friends*

before Christmas, until an appointment on December 26 would give us the results. It was a pretty stressful time for him and me: decorating the house, having our oldest son help him string the outside lights wondering if he would have to do it next year without his father. It was very poignant.

Having worked in Workers' Compensation for many years, Bob had access to numerous medical books, and he was trying to figure out what it could be. Hodgkin's? Leukemia?

On the twenty-sixth he really wanted me with him for the talk with the doctor. When he heard that it was lymphoma, my husband said "How long do I have? I have young children, the youngest being six." The doctor reassured him that it would likely be a chronic thing, coming and going over the years.

Well, after many pills, radiation, and the best intravenous therapy we could find in Ohio, he had a year's grace, then wham, it was back as bad as ever. And that's when he investigated hospitals that had much to do with treating lymphoma, and he started going to a hospital in New York City. He'd fly in every three weeks for drug treatment, but he gradually got weaker and weaker.

His doctor finally wanted him to come and be hospitalized. He was there a week or so when the doctor called me and said that this time things were much more critical.

I flew to New York and for two weeks came to the hospital every day. I was able to visit Bob, but he was sedated and didn't know I was there.

Finally, one lovely, memorable day after they tried reducing some of his medication, Bob responded by squeezing my hand slightly, and then I leaned close and said, "Hi, hon. Here I am, your Slovak princess." (Silly private joke.) "How's about blinking your eyes if you know I'm here?" And he did! And after some gentle kisses from me, I said, "Well, you know how much I love you. How's about a blink if you love me?" And his eyelashes fluttered, and fluttered, and fluttered, and it was lovely, loving, and being loved.

So, what surprises do we find in a given day? Pressed flowers in a book, children's drawings and poems, the cry of a newborn child, and a Slovak princess.

# *Ah, the Girlfriend*

❧

$B$y October of my third year in grammar school I was
convinced that Arleen Sullivan was in love with me. She said,
as we stood in line for our coats that afternoon, "Hi Chris."
She knew my name!

Arleen Sullivan had freckles, blue eyes, nursery-rhyme hair,
curled and brown, good for a gold comb or the moon's light.

A nine-year-old boy doesn't think about the moonlight
mingling with the hair of a beautiful woman, but I did know
back then that Arleen just wasn't Johnny or Jack or some
afternoon in the tree fort shooting off firecrackers or eating
marmalade sandwiches, which, for some reason, my older
brother thought was the right thing to eat deep in the woods
of 1960.

Sometime in November I went food shopping with my
mother and father. I know it was a Friday afternoon, because
my parents always went food shopping on Friday afternoon at
the same supermarket: Grandway, the store in a store where
televisions, mops, bananas, ironing boards, Ovaltine, and
lobster could all be bought in a single afternoon under the
same roof.

Shopping in Grandway was like going on an Australian
walkabout: pick out a cart with straight wheels, walk past the
pyramid of Schaffer Beer, greet Mr. Santini at the fruit and

vegetable aisle, haggle over the price for the bruised bananas and extra-ripe grapes Mr. Santini kept aside for my father, beg my mother to let me push the cart "and I won't zoom down the aisle and ride piggy back on the cart like I did last month, crashing into the Bosco chocolate syrup display."

Between hunting for the right can of tuna (the one with the fish on the label that wore sunglasses while relaxing on a hammock) and weighing out the chestnuts my mother bought that week, my father treated me to an ice-cream sundae over at the snack bar, just beyond the cereal aisle. We men both liked chocolate with an extra scoop of sprinkles generously spread over the top of the dish.

After we finished eating, I spun around on the stool a few times until I was dizzy, then I stepped off, following my father as he began looking for my mother.

I, still a bit wobbly from my spin on the stool, pretended I was Superman walking on top of a blimp and any minute the blimp would explode killing all aboard unless I was able to secure the patch over the gaping hole just out of my reach. I was about to make a dramatic lunge, when I saw, down the aisle, Arleen Sullivan with her mother and father. She waved. I waved. She turned the corner and disappeared, and then the blimp exploded.

"Chris, wipe the chocolate sprinkles from the corner of your mouth," my father said as he spotted my mother picking out a TV guide.

I had a secret.

In mid December, Mrs. Buttress, our third grade teacher, announced that we would be having a Christmas party. "We all have to bring something for the party. Raise your hand when I go down the list. Who will bring in paper plates? Amanda. Napkins? Joe. Plastic glasses? Mary." There were fifty-three children in our class that year. I probably volunteered to bring in a bag of potato chips.

# Friends

On the day of the party we all stepped into the classroom carrying our contributions to the party.

"Everyone settle down." Mrs. Buttress said as she began handing out napkins for everyone. "Open your napkins on your desk. Each person who has something, will you please walk around the classroom and hand out what you brought."

One girl began distributing cups. A boy counted out five M&M's per person. I walked around and let everyone grab a handful of chips from my bag.

We were nearly ready to begin the party. I was already sitting when the door to our room opened and in stepped Arleen Sullivan carrying a tray. Sitting on the tray were twenty-five marshmallow Santa Claus treats. Each was identical: the bodies were made with two large, fat marshmallows held together with toothpicks. The arms and heads were smaller marshmallows also kept in place with toothpicks. Sitting on the top of each white Santa Claus was a small, red paper hat rolled from thick paper, and pressed on the tip of each hat was the smallest marshmallow.

I wanted a marshmallow Santa Claus.

Arleen began handing out the treat, beginning at the first row closest to the door. Obviously she didn't have enough for the entire class. Up and down the rows she went, lifting a Santa Claus and placing it on the desk of this friend and that.

By the time she reached the fourth row, she had ten Santas. By the end of the fifth row she had six. Arleen turned to the sixth row, and soon enough she had five marshmallow Santas left, then five, and then three. She then began walking down my row, the last one beside the window. Arleen picked up the second to the last Santa Claus and handed it to Kathy, then she slowly lifted the last one, the last, white, marshmallow Santa Claus that she, Arleen Sullivan, had made with her own hands. She looked to her right. She took a few steps. She turned in my direction.

"Remember, I saved you from the exploding blimp," I wanted to shout out. Arleen picked up the Santa and placed him gently on my desk. She smiled and licked her fingers.

"Let's sing 'Joy to the World' before we eat," Mrs. Buttress suggested. I am sure that I sang the loudest that December morning thirty-six years ago.

After the song, as everyone began eating, I quickly took my marshmallow Santa Claus, wrapped him in my napkin, and stashed him in my book bag.

On the way home in the bus, I pulled Santa out from the bag and held him in my cupped hands as if he were Tinker Bell, or Kryptonite . . . something delicate, capable of joining me on my adventure, and full of enough power to kill a man of steel, especially if his sister discovered what he had and why he was keeping it.

Mercifully my sister was out ice-skating with Patty down the street when I arrived home, and my mother thought I made the marshmallow Santa as some sort of school project. "Hang your coat. There's a Christmas card on your dresser from your grandmother. Your father will be home early tonight."

I ran up the stairs, stepped into my room, and closed the door behind me. After I read my grandmother's card, and stuffed the five-dollar bill into my pocket, I placed my marshmallow Santa Claus on the top of my dresser, in the very middle, just below the mirror. He sat there like Buddha.

For weeks I worshiped that little man created in Arleen Sullivan's kitchen while she breathed on him, pricked him with tooth picks, rolled the small paper in her hands to make a hat. Arleen Sullivan, the girl with the brown hair and freckles. That Santa Claus was the first thing I looked at when I woke up in the morning, and the last thing I looked at before I turned off my lights at night.

## Friends

Do you know what happens to marshmallows if they sit on a dresser in the open air for several months? The begin to shrink, wrinkle, dry up like a prune.

One day after school, as I stepped into the house, my mother said, "Chris, I did some heavy cleaning in your room today." That is all she had to say. I flew up the stairs faster than Superman. My mother had tossed out the dried marshmallow Santa Claus, but she had left, sitting on the dresser, the small red paper hat Arleen had rolled between her fingertips somewhere long ago when Clark Kent was just a cub reporter.

When I was nine years old I had a greater secret than marmalade and firecrackers.

# Wife as Best Friend

❧

$W$hen I fly across the country to give a talk, I often like to strike up a conversation with the person sitting next to me. I've met sales people from major corporations, Air Force pilots, lawyers, grandmothers. If I meet people in professions that I do not know very much about, I like to ask if they have any stories that they remember, that stick in their minds for one reason or another.

On a recent trip to California I sat beside a retired family doctor. He was on his way to San Francisco for a month with his grandchildren.

After the initial introductions, and the usually chit-chat, I asked the man if he has any patients he remembers, or any incident that stands out in his mind. He shared two stories with me. The first was about the tigers in the teacup.

According to my new doctor friend, there seemed to be a problem in his town with an old woman. She refused to pay her taxes, and no one knew what to do with her.

She was given warnings in the mail; the police knocked on her front door. Even her sister, who was a few years younger than the old woman, tried to convince her sister how important taxes were.

The old woman was ninety-five, according to the doctor. She was raking leaves one day in October when she looked up at the trees and then fell to the ground.

# Friends

"I was on my way to the hospital," the doctor said, "driving through her street, when I saw Miss Hannah lying on the leaves.

"The woman was still breathing by the time I stopped the car and ran to her side. I lifted her into my arms. She was lighter than a bag of feathers, and I began to carry her to her house."

The doctor sitting next to me was a big man, and obviously once strong.

"As I was carrying Miss Hannah," the doctor said, " she whispered, soft and easy, 'There are tigers in my teacup,' and then she smiled. I said in a polite way, 'Yes, Miss Hannah.' Then she asked me to look at all the colors of the leaves, how beautiful they were, especially the yellow leaves, and then she died, right in my arms."

We can all easily understand the power of sadness and how, in an odd way, such feelings coat our lives with a satisfying sheen, like the wetness after a severe rain storm. The thunder and lightning can be powerful, frightening, even the cause of discomfort, but after the rain, there is a silence, a slow return to stillness that defines all things in the context of what we know and remember.

The doctor said that when he placed Miss Hannah on her couch and called the preacher and her family, he stayed around until everyone came who needed to. "As I was waiting" he said, "I walked into Miss Hannah's kitchen, and I saw, sitting in the middle of her kitchen table, a small teacup, and in the teacup were several flowers, tiger lilies, fresh and yellow and arranged with care. Tigers in her teacup."

Because the doctor saw how interested I was in his first story, especially after I asked him if I could take notes and use his story in a book someday, he offered another one.

"I had a camel once," he said. "You know, a camel, from the desert. I had fixed up the broken leg of a prince, or something, from a wealthy Egyptian family.

"You see, my wife and I were on vacation to see the pyramids. We were shopping in one of the markets. It was wonderful: tents, flowers, fancy nuts and figs for sale, brass horns, people dressed in beautiful silk.

"We were looking at some blankets, when we heard a loud cry, a man's cry. A crowd formed, so my wife and I walked across the street to investigate.

"There had been an accident. A boy had run to look at the parrots. There were many cages under a tent. Inside each cage were beautiful birds. They didn't seem real: pink, yellow, blue. This boy had run from his father and had been struck by a car. The father was the one who screamed out. I couldn't speak the language, but everyone quickly understood that I was a doctor.

"We carried the boy under one of the tents. It was a very hot day. You could smell the desert. No matter what time of day, there was this breeze, a friendly, slow breeze, and there was a smell of flowers and dust and dryness. The boy's leg was broken, so he was taken to the hospital. I stayed with him and was able to help set his leg after x-rays were taken.

"That night, my wife and I had dinner in a restaurant that looked like the insides of a pharaoh's palace. When we arrived at our hotel, the manager bowed down before me. I was embarrassed. He led my wife and me to the courtyard. There, eating the grass, was a tall, plump, brown camel. It had a blanket on its back, gold tassels hanging from both sides of its head. The reins were silver, and there were hundreds of little bells tied to the camel's saddle.

"'This camel is a gift,' the manager said, 'from the boy's father. You saved his son, and he wished to give you this gift to take back to America so that when you ride to children's homes, they will know you are an important doctor.'"

The doctor smiled at me and said, "Can you see me riding down the streets of New York on a camel? My wife suggested we give the camel to our guide, who had a large family. At the end of our trip that is what we did, but not before my wife suggested we clip off one of the little bells and keep it as a souvenir. I tied the bell to my bag and kept it there until the day I retired."

"What happened to the bell?" I asked.

"I put it in my wife's coffin when she died."

# Sister as Friend

W hat is this stuff?" I asked as I grabbed a wad of earth. Anne turned her attention away from the raspberries we were picking and said, "Clay, I think. Hey, this is clay! We're standing in a gully runoff. After each rain a bit of this stuff collects. Over time a natural clay is made. See?" Anne grabbed some of the clay in her hands and squeezed the lump until it began to ooze out between her fingers.

Anne wiggled her hand into the soft earth. After she scooped up some of the clay, she began to roll it and knead it, and quick enough it began to look and feel like clay. "Let's get a bucket!"

Children seem to have a natural sense of adventure, or at least for the start of an adventure. No one asked Anne what she needed a bucket for. Obviously she wanted to collect clay. No one asked the next question. The immediate idea was to dig up some of the natural clay and drop it into a bucket, which I found inside the chicken coop. By the time I returned with the bucket, Anne had already created a foot-high mound of our clay.

"That's enough," I said. We bent down to our labor and filled the bucket with the moist, elastic earth.

"Now what?" I asked.

# Friends

"Let's take this back to the chicken coop." Anne tugged at the bucket's handle, but the burden was too heavy for her. I grabbed one side of the handle, and she pulled on the other. Together we walked through the woods and up to the chicken coop.

The chicken coop was a pale-green building that never housed any chickens in my lifetime. On some days the chicken coop was Long John Silver's pirate ship; on other days it was John Wayne's saloon, or Robin Hood's secret hideout. Most days it was just a chicken coop.

"Let's pretend we're bakers," Anne suggested.

"I don't want to be an old baker." I turned, faced my sister, and pulled my eyelids back and rolled my eyes so that I looked like a monster with white eyeballs.

"You never want to be what I want to be!" Anne nearly socked me.

"Okay, we'll be bakers. Why don't we turn the barrel upside down and use the top as our baker's table?" I suggested.

Anne and I had found, the summer before, a real barrel, like the old-fashioned apple barrel Jim Hawkins hid in when he overheard Long John Silver's plan of mutiny.

We dragged the bucket of clay into the baker's shop. We quickly turned the barrel upside down, then Anne reached into the bucket and slapped a fistful of clay onto the barrel top. "We need a rolling pin."

I ran out and returned in less than a minute with a glass soda bottle. "Here. Use this."

Anne grabbed the bottle and began rolling out the clay. "Let's make cookies."

We tried to cut round cookies from the flat clay with sticks we picked up from the floor. Then we tried making them by simply using our fingers as knives, but that didn't work either.

"We need a cookie cutter." Anne said.

I looked toward the house. My grandfather was kneeling in the rose garden. My grandmother was sitting on a lawn chair reading the newspaper. I stood up and slowly walked toward the back porch.

When my grandfather looked up from his flowers, I waved. He squinted his eyes, then returned to his weeding. My grandmother never looked up from her newspaper.

Within a few seconds I was in the kitchen, opening the third drawer of the cabinet, reaching in and grabbing a cookie cutter. My mother ignored me. I stuffed the cutter into my pocket, then I ran out the back door. My grandmother approached the house just as I took a flying leap over the stairs. Midway down she looked up and caught a glimpse of a flashing figure, Batman perhaps, escaping the near fatal discovery. My grandmother continued walking up the stairs as I ran back to the chicken coop.

"Did you get it?" Anne asked as she wiped her forehead with her muddy hand.

"Yeah!" I pulled the cookie cutter from my pocket.

"That's not a cookie cutter," she laughed. "That's a doughnut cutter." It had a small red handle and a metal form attached in the shape of a doughnut.

"Well, let's make doughnuts."

Anne wrinkled her dirty forehead. "Chrissy. We're making cookies."

"Cookies? Doughnuts? What difference does it make?" I argued.

"I don't like doughnuts," Anne firmly stated. "They always taste uncooked."

I looked at my sister, ready to say that she was out of her mind or just plain stupid. I did make an attempt at saying that we were just pretending, and pretend doughnuts never tasted uncooked, but she began to wind up her face into an Anne fit, so I just said "Okay. Okay. We'll make cookies." I inspected the doughnut cutter and noticed that the center hole could be unclipped from the main piece of metal. I twisted the doughnut hole portion out of the handle. "There. Happy? Now we can use this to make nice round cookies."

I was about to throw away the small doughnut hole part, when Anne suggested, "Let's make penny cookies."

"What?" I asked. By now I was lingering at the door, considering the cherries that hung from the tree beyond the green fence.

"Penny cookies. We can use the doughnut hole maker and make us some penny cookies. You know, cookies the size of pennies?"

"Anne! That's a waste of time. We can make many big cookies. It'll take forever to make small ones." I was quickly losing interest in the whole idea and edging toward the cherry tree.

"We can make plenty of penny cookies. What's the difference? I like how small they'll look." Anne jabbed the doughnut hole cutter into the flat clay and pulled out a single mud cookie, a penny cookie. She held it in the flat of her brown hand. "See?"

"Want some cherries?" I yelled out as I hung upside down in the cherry tree.

"Chrissy, you come back here! You're an old goat." Anne was about to toss the clay back into the bucket and forget the whole thing, when I thought of a new twist to our pretend.

I jumped out of the tree and said, "Anne, you make the cookies and I'll bake them."

She began to regain interest. "How can we bake them. We don't have a stove."

"Yes we do. Look outside."

Anne looked out the front door of the chicken coop. "All I see is the stupid garage."

"Yeah, but look how bright the sun is."

"So what."

"The sun, Anne. It's hot out today. After you cut out the penny cookies, we can carry them up to the roof and lay them out in rows. The sun will bake them. We'll pretend the roof is our oven."

"How many penny cookies do you think we can make?" Anne asked.

"Maybe a hundred, I guess."

"Can we make a thousand?"

I wasn't sure we could count that high. "Sure. A thousand. We can do that."

So we began. Anne stood behind the barrel like a baker, rolling out the mud with her soda bottle, then stomping the doughnut hole cutter into the "dough." When she finished making a cookie she placed it on a wide board we found leaning against the wall. That was our baker's tray. Each time the tray was full, I carried the cookies to the roof.

We had built a ladder the summer before and leaned it against the side of the chicken coop. That ladder was great for escaping the Sheriff of Nottingham.

After I climbed to the roof, I placed each tray of penny cookies in a neat row. Each row was made up of ten cookies, which made it easy for me to keep track.

In two hours we had made 500 cookies. An hour later the fire whistle blew at noon. Sarah and I had finished 732 cookies. By the time my mother called us in for a late lunch, we had created 907 cookies. We were anxious to reach our goal, so we stayed at our work another twenty minutes.

"Nine-hundred and ninety-seven. Nine-hundred and ninety-eight. Nine-hundred and ninety-nine. One-thousand!" Anne and I yelled out together as we jumped up and down and hugged each other.

"Lunch!" my mother called out from a world we had long forgotten.

## Friends

Coming!" Anne answered. "You bring this last batch to the roof. I'll go inside and wash up. We did it."

It is, in part, because of my sister Anne that I learned what it means to love, to play, to enjoy the sun, to have my sister as a friend; important lessons that I have carried with me for all of my life. You would have loved the taste of those penny cookies.

# The Love of a Friend

❦

Often I am asked to speak to young people about what is important in life. Of course, I learned early on that we all have to answer this question for ourselves, but it seems to me that we adults can offer hints to young people, hints about the significance of living a reflective life in the face of the many, many questions we are confronted with no matter how old we are.

When I was a graduate student at Columbia University, I was walking through the campus past one of the academic buildings when a young woman opened the door and walked down the stairs to the sidewalk. I knew her name was Kathy because she was in one of my classes. The class had, perhaps, a hundred students, and Kathy sat in the front, one of the few who spoke up, and what she had to say was often clever, usually insightful as she garnered the admiration of the professor and the envy of everyone else.

Kathy looked like a young Ali McGraw. Her hair was black. Her wide eyes and smile illuminated her face and expressed her beauty and intellect when she spoke or laughed.

As she stepped to the sidewalk, she and I walked together and, to be polite, I introduced myself.

"We're in class together. My name is Chris."

"I'm Kathy,"

"Yes. I know."

She turned and smiled. "Where are you heading?"

"There's a Charlie Chaplin movie being shown over at the Barnard Auditorium."

We spoke about the class, about the books we were reading for the course, and by the time we came to the intersection, I sheepishly asked, "Would you like to see the movie?"

Kathy turned to me and said, simply, "Yes."

She and I walked over to the college and watched the Little Tramp jiggle and dance, smile and frown as he twirled his cane, won the heart of the girl, and waddled into the happy distance of the fading movie screen.

Back on the street, Kathy said that she had enjoyed the film, and she had to go home. She lived in the Village.

"I'll take you home," I suggested. "It's late."

Kathy did not protest. We entered the subway system, stood in a crowded car. After many stops, we came to Kathy's street. We both stepped out. I walked her home. At the entrance to her building she thanked me, we shook hands, and I was on my way.

Kathy and I dated for the next few months. She and I drove to one of her job interviews in Connecticut in her yellow Volkswagen. She and I spent an evening at her house watching television. She joined me in my dorm as we read poetry and kissed. She brought me to her parents' house in New Jersey where we washed her car and lay out in the sun on the roof of her house. This young woman was strong, smart, beautiful. She was not afraid to express her affection emotionally and physically. I just wasn't falling in love with her.

I was determined as a young man to pursue relationships with women in a way that would always bring honesty and goodness and joy. I knew the feeling, but I could not explain it. I knew that as a friendship developed with a woman, often such a friendship moved slowly toward a time when decisions had to be made: is this love or is this friendship? Is this developing into a future, or is this developing into entertainment?

Time and time again the issue of sexuality arose, and for me it was always connected with love. I wanted to be in love. I wanted emotional and physical stability and joy and excitement, and I thought that without the emotional embrace, the physical embrace would be empty, just as I felt that the emotional embrace without the physical embrace was also empty.

We are a part of the world, and all things have various divisions. For us, we have an inside self and an outside self, the human and the spiritual, the soul part and the body part, the voice and the silence.

Kathy and I got along just fine. She wanted the relationship to blossom. She wanted to combine our physical joys with our emotional joys. She was honest with her body, with her gifts, with her self, but I just knew there was no future for us.

Who can explain such a feeling? We all have this inner voice, this little whisper that seems to guide us, that seems to nudge us, that seems to help us along the way. Bright, beautiful, aggressive, sexy, honest Kathy and I met after class. As she and I walked through the campus toward my dorm, she handed me a brown paper bag. "I made you lunch."

She handed me the heavy bag.

"I made a chicken salad sandwich. I know you like that. And I added a chocolate doughnut and a Coke." Kathy was thoughtful, generous, charming.

I thanked her for the lunch and held it in my right hand. Kathy took my left hand in hers as we continued to walk toward my dorm.

"Let's spend some time together," she suggested as she squeezed my hand a bit. It felt so fine and warm and strong.

"Kathy," I said. "I don't think we should see each other any longer. I am not falling in love with you."

# Friends

She stopped, looked at me, turned her head slightly, let go of my hand, and just walked away. I never saw her again. As I continued walking toward my building, I dropped the lunch into a trash can and felt relieved.

Now, twenty-four years later, I am still thinking about Kathy, hoping I didn't hurt her, wishing there was something I could have done to spare her the look of sadness that entered those beautiful eyes. I have been rejected in my life plenty of times, by women, at job interviews, by editors. I know what stings the eyes when we are turned down. But I have also come to realize that each time I have come to a crossroads in my life, that each time I have to, once again, knock at the door of my future, I have to endure the rejection, that many doors won't open, that my sense of hope and optimism is challenge each time I come to a new door.

I wish I could find Kathy and tell her what she meant to me. She came into my life at a time when I was lonely and a bit defeated. She was the smartest person in class, and the prettiest, and she made the professor laugh, and she liked me. I think she was falling in love with me.

I am sure such a person is doing just fine. I am sure she is a successful college professor somewhere. (That was one of her dreams.) I am sure she is a wonderful mother. (Another one of her goals.) I am also sure that she is a whole, vibrant, sexy, wonderful, bright, and honest wife too.

I regret not keeping in touch with Kathy, and not eating those delicious chicken salad sandwiches and chocolate doughnuts when they were placed in my hands honestly, with courage and joy. I didn't realize that I gave up a friend.

# Tokens of Friendship

❧

I linger over shadows and accept their distorted imitation of reality. Abstract painters work with such distortions, seeing the face of a woman, let's say as Picasso used to do, then turning such a face sideways, adding a view from the back, combining odd shapes where ears must go when it is really the place for an eye, never the woman but the hint of a woman, someone new perhaps, a second reality to be hung in the museums to be admired.

There are shadows outside my window, oak trees, streams of ink blots spreading out on the grass, across the road, up against my neighbor's house. There is a white chair sitting on the deck and a long, dark silhouette of a chair drawn by the eastern sun on the floor beams.

Perhaps it is dangerous to love the semblance of things. We wear clothes to protect our essential physical selves, but often the clothes become the person, the mask, the hint of what can be seen and loved, and then such hidden arms and breasts become the form to fill the cut of a dress or the bulge of a shirt, and that is all. We love the image but not the authenticity.

One of the most profound tokens of friendship I ever received was in response to a moment's gesture. I have a friend I met through my writing. She recognized herself in my books, the clear, essential self of her life as a wife, mother, and teacher, and she wrote me a letter telling me so. Such is the power of words, such is the renunciation of shadows and the embrace of what is supple when we read a book that surrounds our bodies and souls with the honey of truth that we have tasted.

We corresponded, this young woman and I, and we quickly learned that we saw and felt the same things in what we read, in the way we bounce our hands on the tops of bushes, in the way we smell a magnolia blossom, and in what we recognized as the essential qualities of a courageous life built on love and faith.

I was in Chicago giving a talk about my books, about writing, about living a reflective life. After the evening was complete, after the reception and the book signings, I returned to my hotel room tired but pleased. I called Roe and wrote out a few postcards.

As I sat at the desk in my room, my hand rested upon the pad of yellow note paper I had brought and, on a whim, I traced the outline of my hand as I use to do when I was in elementary school. The pen tickled as it traced the contours of my fingers: up and around and down and back up again and down, around the thumb and back down to my wrist. The next morning I sent my hand print to my writing friend.

Two weeks later I received the same yellow piece of paper from my friend with her own hand print outlined inside of mine. The intimation of the other, the semblance of two hands. The extended hands in an embrace is a universal sign of trust and friendship.

I will never forget the picture I saw in a history book that discussed the dropping of the atomic bomb on Hiroshima and Nagasaki. There was a wall, and on this wall was the vague shadow of a person. The bomb exploded with such power and force that it vaporized the person on the sidewalk, at the same time burning the person's shadow onto the wall.

Where is Peter Pan's shadow? In eastern countries, peasants still believe that the shadow of a menstruating woman can wither flowers and strangle trees. Time is connected to shadows in the angle of the sundial. Perhaps grief is the substance of shadows: what is left behind in the displacement of what is loved. Doubt crouched in a valley? An unseen power? Swollen sails in a distant sea?

Ghosts have no shadows. I linger over the shadows and seek the solid forms: the round, the slender, the soft, the warm. I prefer Degas to Picasso, laughter to silence, water to dust.

Who can live with only the charcoal outline of self, fearful of the body, at a loss about how to refine the intellect? I cannot—that is why I am grateful for the reality of my family and my friends, people I love who trick the shadows with magnolia blossoms, and who place their hands into the palm of my real, open hand.

# Brother as Friend

❦

When I was eight years old, I already knew that my older brother, Bruno, was Merlin, Davy Crockett, or Thomas Edison. Bruno, who was fourteen at the time, was always planning an adventure in the woods: building a tree fort, baking apples in the campfire, creating raked paths from one end of my father's property to the next. My sisters and brothers and I pretended that we were Robin Hood's merry men, foot soldiers in the American Revolution, or friends of the clever Swamp Fox, who looked exactly like my brother Bruno. He was the master of the imagination. He created the day's events and games in our home when we were all children.

Bruno was also an inventor. It was Bruno who built a pulley system from the top lawn to the lower fields, a contraption of ropes and wheels and a small platform where we transported secret notes back and forth, from one end of our imagination to the other. It was Bruno who built a catapult, good for lobbing into the woods the crab apples that accumulated on the lawn under the apple tree that Bruno said looked like an elephant. And it was Bruno who built from scratch a wooden airplane with green wings, a red body, and a wood propeller that turned when it was pushed through the air. I wanted that wooden airplane.

My brother kept this plane on the top shelf of his bookcase in his room, out of reach from little boys of eight. One afternoon, while my brother was shopping with my father, I crept into his room, pulled a chair across the floor, climbed to the top of the dresser, reached up as far as I could, and just managed to grab hold of the right wing of the airplane. I quickly slid down and sat on the floor flying the plane around the world, as I felt the smooth wood in my hands, as I watched the small propeller twirl and twirl.

"What are you doing, you old goat?" Bruno growled as he stood in the doorway of his room. He had returned from his shopping trip.

"I'm playing with my airplane," I said, convinced that this little toy really did, somehow, belong to me.

"I put it on the shelf to keep it from your grubby hands." Bruno yanked the airplane from me, reached up and returned it to the top shelf, where the propeller immediately stopped rotating.

"Can't I play with it?" not daring to ask the bigger question.

"No. I made it. It's mine. You'd break it."

I walked out of his room.

That night, as my mother was adjusting my blanket before I slept, I asked her if she had had a favorite toy when she was little.

"My doll Denise."

"Was it always yours?" I asked.

"Yes, my mother gave it to me for my birthday."

"I like airplanes," I said. "Bruno made an airplane with green wings and a propeller. He called me an old goat."

"Bruno loves you very much," my mother said.

"He lets me wear his Davy Crockett hat," I said. "And we sleep together in the tree fort. And he let me play with his submarine in the bathtub."

"Did you ask Bruno if you could have the airplane for keeps?"

"No. I just took it from his shelf to play with it."

"Christopher, sometimes you have to let people know exactly what you are thinking."

"You mean he doesn't really know that I want to have the plane for me?"

"Probably not. Why don't you see what he might say tomorrow?"

I looked at my mother in the half darkness. "Good night, my little pilot," she said.

The next morning I ran to Bruno's room and jumped on his bed. He was not yet awake. "Can I have it? Can I have it for keeps?"

Bruno stirred from his sleep. "What are you talking about, Chrissy?"

"The airplane. Can I have it for keeps? I love that plane."

He looked at me suddenly.

"I like how the propeller spins," I said sheepishly.

Bruno slipped from his bed, reached up to the top of his shelf, and pulled down the airplane. "Here, Chrissy. You can have it for keeps. You can also push the wheels up and down." Then he showed me how the wheels moved for landing and take-off.

I looked up at him. "For keeps?" I asked.

"Yep, you old goat, for keeps."

I will never forget running out of his room with the plane, watching the propeller twirl and twirl down the hall with me as I ran to show my mother.

# The Friendship of the Father

❧

Are we supposed to be hunters and gatherers? Are we in the world to hide from our primitive selves: folding napkins after a meal, strolling up and down the florescent food market chatting with a neighbor, weighing the difference between hamburger and steak?

There is a dynamic difference between the man I am today and the man I would have been if it were not for my father and grandfather, shadows of a warning that I dare not step across the line or I will fall back into centuries of savagery and lost faith.

During World War I my grandfather was shot in his left arm. His injury was so extensive and violent that he begged the doctors not to cut off his arm. When he woke up a few hours later, following the operation, my grandfather slowly reached with his right arm down along his left shoulder, his elbow, and yes, the rest of his arm. Although the doctors did not cut off his arm, they were helpless in their attempt to restore any usefulness. For the rest of his life, my grandfather's left arm was a hanging appendage.

Though he died thirty years ago, I still see my grandfather planting roses in the backyard, struggling with the shovel, wiggling the small plant into place, and scooping up the dirt with the shovel and his strong, good arm. I see him lifting a queen of hearts and snapping it onto the kitchen table top as he and I played Follow the Suit.

My grandfather could dust off his past adventures with a quick sweep of his good hand and extend the memory of a Europe in the savage grip of the Nazi occupation, how he spent time in a prisoner-of-war camp, how he escaped to England, how he was separated from my grandmother and mother for four years, all, all bits of story and anguish contained in the memory of a man who wore a white shirt on Sunday and stood on the back lawn surveying the progress of the garden flowers.

Today I look at my own father. He is eighty-five. He too came from the place of a distant roar, that past where young soldiers were catapulted from canvas and steel gliders down along the side of a meadow in the heart of Belgium, that past where his mother died young and loneliness was contained in his heart as he wrote books of poetry, danced in the ballrooms of evenings lost, and met my mother in Paris while World War II was just about finished gouging out the flesh of a Europe that could no longer protect itself with guns and spears. A new beast rose up from the smoke and dust, the atomic blast, the mane of the savage lion erupting over the veldt of our once innocent selves.

My father sailed upon the Mediterranean, made his way through the streets of Manhattan, worked for forty years in stoic acceptance and pride writing books, teaching, translating, tending to his six children, and dreaming of home where young men flew down a meadow and Paris contained the new hope of victory and his bride.

Fathers contain the savage and tame worlds within themselves. I was the lucky grandson to feel the strength of my grandfather's good hand on my shoulder as he urged me off to bed with a blessing and good wishes. I was the lucky son to hear the voice of my father as he defined gentleness in his insistence that we read and pray and contain ourselves as gentlemen in the face of a world that is always on the brink of savagery.

I wonder what my three children see when they come to me with their cards and greetings of "Happy Father's Day"?

# The Friendship of the Mother

~

Mothers seem to know how to help their children at just
the right moment. They don't learn these things in school.
They just seem to see things, and know what to say and do.

One afternoon, when I was a boy, I heard a squealing
sound emanating from the woods. I was sitting on the back
porch reading a Superman comic book when there was a
sudden, piercing cry. I loosened my Clark Kent tie and turned
my head just in time to see Moses, our cat, run out from under
the tangled brush with a young rabbit dangling from its jaws.

"Moses!" I screamed. "Moses!" I jumped up from my chair,
flew over Metropolis and down the five steps. I used my x-ray
vision, ran across the lawn, and chased the cat into the
garage, where it reluctantly dropped the rabbit beside the front
wheel of my bicycle. The cat quickly ran out of the garage as I
leaned over and scooped up the limp rabbit into my hands.

"Mom," I said through my Superman tears as I entered the
kitchen, "Moses killed a rabbit."

"Now don't give up hope so quickly, Christopher," she said
as she leaned over and slowly stroked the small creature's
head. "Let's get a box and some straw."

"But it's dead. Moses killed it!" I said with conviction.

"First we have to wait and see, Chris. We have to do the
best we can and wait and see."

My mother and I found a shoe box and filled the box with dry, brown bits of grass we gathered in the garden, then we placed the box beside the radiator in the kitchen and placed the rabbit on its side on the new, soft, little bed. And then I extended my arms before me and flew out onto the back porch where I continued reading about Clark Kent and Lois Lane.

"Christopher! Lunch!" my mother called a bit later. I stood up, tossed the comic book onto the chair, and ran inside the kitchen. I saw that the shoe box was no longer beside the radiator. I didn't see it anywhere until I stepped up to the kitchen table. There on my chair was the shoe box, and inside the box was a five-inch, brown rabbit sitting up with confidence nibbling the edge of a wide piece of fresh lettuce.

"See, my Superman, what can happen sometimes if you are patient and persistent?" my mother said as she sat at the table. She and I had soup and lots and lots of fresh lettuce for lunch that afternoon, and six weeks later we carried a cage to the center of the woods and released a fat, healthy rabbit where, perhaps, Alice would someday find it during her adventures in wonderland, or at least that is what my mother said.

How is it that mothers have this special vision, not x-ray vision like Superman, but this ability to see what children need? How does a mother learn how to help her children see things in a special way? It seems to me mothers just seem to know, like magic.

One afternoon in October, when I was in first grade, the teacher explained to the class that the next day we were going to be making an art project with leaves. The plan was for us to gather leaves and place them under wax paper and make a collage to celebrate autumn. I remember the teacher saying at the end of the class, "Be sure you collect some beautiful leaves."

## Friends

I walked home that afternoon with my book bag, my homework, and my tears. As I walked along the sidewalk, I was gravely disappointed with what I saw: brown leaves, split leaves, leaves with bumps and stains. I couldn't find a leaf that was even close to being beautiful. By the time I stepped into the house, I was discouraged and destined to receive a poor grade in art.

"Christopher?" my mother asked. "What is the matter?"

"I'm supposed to find some beautiful leaves for tomorrow's art class, and I walked all the way home, and I didn't see any."

My mother gave me that don't-give-up talk again as she helped me with my book bag. "Let's see if I can help you." She stepped up to the kitchen cabinet, pulled out a brown bag with handles, and said, "Let's go outside and see what we can find."

My mother held my hand as we both stepped along the back porch and walked down the stairs onto the small bit of lawn. At the very first leaf we came upon my mother stooped down and pointed. "Look Christopher. Look at the edge of this leaf. How pretty it is, like the fins of a fish."

I picked up the beautiful leaf and placed it carefully into my bag.

We came upon another leaf.

"Christopher. Look how beautiful. Look at the veins in this leaf, like the veins in our hands." She traced the veins in my right hand with her index finger. It tickled. I laughed, and then I placed the second beautiful leaf into my bag.

My mother and I must have gathered fifty leaves that afternoon. Every leaf to my mother was beautiful, and by the end of the week, I received an A+ on my leaf collage.

A mother who knows how to help her children see things with a refined vision can create a world of goodness from frightened rabbits and beautiful leaves.

With her strength and mom-power I learned that optimism and beauty will always protect me, even as I grow older, even as I wear more and more my Clark Kent disguise.

My mother is seventy-five, but she still sees beauty, she still has faith, and she still believes that I am Superman.

# Children as Friends

I will return to the days when my hair was long and my dreams were entwined with the smell of waxed floors and the voice of teenagers calling out, "Hi, Mr. de Vinck." "Good morning, Mr. de Vinck." "I did my reading last night in *To Kill a Mockingbird*, Mr. de Vinck, the part about Scout rolling into the Radley yard and Atticus telling them to leave the Radley place alone. I liked that."

I was a twenty-three-year old man when I wrote *Mr. de Vinck* on the blackboard for the first time. I laughed as I stood before my very first students. "All my life this name was my father. Today is the first time I am known to anyone as Mr. de Vinck."

"Can't we just call you Chris?," a boy in the back row asked.

I was tempted to say yes, but I knew from the very first day that students were not to be my disciples or friends. I knew from the first day of teaching that my time with the boys and girls was temporary, that no matter how close I came to these children, I would have to let them go in June, to let them go forever, as they forgot me but not Atticus, or Juliet, or Huck Finn calling out to Jim. No, my intention as a teacher from the very beginning was to give the children a flower that does not wilt. I knew about a garden, a certain place. I knew what waits for those who step onto the open earth and plant, what, a seed? A book? An idea?

Real teachers see the inevitability of death in the face of all the students who sit before them in September each year. The teachers who do not see death do not have any idea what to do from season to season with the young people who sit in class. If we know death, we know that there is a time to be filled in between the present and the future. Real teachers do not fill the minds of children with facts. Real teachers fills the children's hearts with sorrow, laughter, anger, humor, doubt, and conviction.

If children learn how to laugh, all history, all math, all science is rooted in a future time when they will become adults and will be able to endure the loneliness or fear or humor or laughter when they are about to perform surgery, or drive a tractor-trailer along Route 80 while their sons sleep and wait in their beds in Iowa or Maine for their fathers to come home.

I stepped into the classroom twenty years ago because I knew there existed a world other than the world of routine, hockey scores, television, popularity, flashy cars, and varsity letters. I knew that unless we are taught how to see beyond the surface of things, we will never know the joy of sorrow, the wisdom of loneliness, the courage of sacrifice, the dignity of poverty, the power of the powerless, the solace in memory, the hope of the future, the conviction of our doubts.

Eternity revolves around F. Scott Fitzgerald's Gatsby and Daisy as they embrace in the garden house in the novel *The Great Gatsby*. Shakespeare's devil, Iago, is smoked out of hiding when Othello finally sees. Jim Burden remembers a time and a place and a prairie and snakes and a girl, his Antonia, and he is glad for the memory. I wanted to teach children to be glad for the memories, to smoke out the devil, to embrace all eternity and dance and dance and dance.

## Friends

Somehow many people stepped over the line into their own awareness, into a world of other: other ways of feeling, other ways of reading, other ways of loving, other ways of praying, other ways of planting a row of daffodils. Many people understand Botticelli, Copland, Shakespeare, the voice of their mothers calling them in to supper. This is the place I knew existed when I became a teacher. "My name is Mr. de Vinck."

A conductor lifts his baton and indicates where to go, at what time, according to the sounds that have taken place and the sounds that are about to take place. From experience, from listening, from weeping and dancing and sleeping and dreaming the conductor stands before a collection of human beings who hold various instruments in their hands. Musicians live their own experiences, their own memories, their own defeats and successes, and so they come to rehearsal. The conductor, with confidence, brings the musicians forward to another place. Unless the whole orchestra walks over to that place of Mozart, or Beethoven, that place the composer created out of his own sadness and joy, out of his own weeping and dreaming, the music will not be reproduced as the composer intended.

Yes. Teacher. Conductor. The musicians sit before him with their rich experiences. Yes. Teacher. He begins the first day of the school year, lifts the baton and begins slowly, note to note, child to child, place to place, word to word always pointing in a direction, nudging, cajoling, encouraging, guiding his students toward what, a door, a path, a place, a feeling, a certitude that there waits for them the possibility of salvation, and I do not mean this in a religious sense exclusively. Students who sit in a classroom in September have the opportunity to be freed from what they don't know, to be sent to a new world that will allow them to grow, or write, or sing, or be. A young man or woman who learns to be still at the end of his or her formal education is a person who has learned much about madness and confusion.

Yes. Teacher. He has the power to say, "Go on, that's the way. You are on the right track, can you feel it? Can you see what Thoreau meant about the water? Can you feel the hunger Richard Wright felt as a child? Can you hold in your arms, at Gettysburg, the dead soldier who has a letter for his son in his pocket? Can you hold the bones of Peking Man in your hands and breathe and breathe and breathe until your lungs pull you in with fear and recognition that in these bones is your past and your destiny?

Yes. Teacher. Teach the children to sit in the Challenger as it explodes. Ask the children what those seven human beings felt as they struggled with the oxygen masks, as the broken machine was falling, falling, and falling into the ocean and then all was silent.

The teacher has the power to take his students outside into the schoolyard where the earth might be soft after a sudden rain. Teacher. Yes, teacher. He asks a girl with new sneakers to press her right foot into the ground. The teacher asks the girl and the class, "What do you see in the mud?"

"Mr. de Vinck, all I see is the footprint of Jenny's Nike sneaker."

Yes. Teacher. "Can you imagine the footprint that is still on the moon? The moon? There are footprints of people, just like you, on the moon." Yes. Teacher. Atticus knew. Mr. Hollands knew. Mr. Chips knew. Annie Sullivan knew. Teacher. Rabbi. Minister. Priest. Father. Mother.

On my first day of school as a teacher I wrote my name on the blackboard and no one laughed except me. You see, my father took me and my brothers and sisters to the corundum mines in central Ontario, Canada. My father was a writer and a teacher, and he said one night on vacation, "I heard there are abandoned corundum mines not far from here. Did you know that corundum is the second hardest material after the diamond?" He picked up a piece of corundum he had on the windowsill of the summer cabin he had built in 1960. "Corundum is so hard it can cut right into glass, just like a diamond," and then he took the piece of rough stone and wrote in neat little letters the names of my sisters and brothers and me, right there in the glass, and then he wrote the date at the bottom of the list, July 18, 1961. I was ten years old. "Tomorrow, we'll go to the corundum mines and look for quartz crystals."

"What is a crystal?" I asked.

"Ah, you will have to find out for yourself. I'll tell you this much. It looks like a diamond, and feels like a diamond, and, well, you'll know when you find one."

The next day my father and mother, my sisters and brothers and I drove along a winding road that eventually turned into a dirt road that eventually ended in a wide meadow. "Now we walk," my father said, and so we walked uphill in the heat, in single file, swatting the mosquitoes. My mother sang French songs. I wanted to find a crystal that looked like a diamond.

In the early part of the century, central Ontario was a major source for corundum crystals used in grinding tools throughout the world. To find the stones, the earth was mined by digging with huge machines and pulling out earth and stones and mountains of rock at the base of the mine. When scientists learned how to create synthetic crystals, there was no more need for corundum, so the mines were abandoned, the huge rock piles left behind. My father knew that such a place was a place to find mica, feldspar, quartz crystals, pyrite, granite.

"Here, here is the pool," my father announced as he called from a distance. The pool was the filled mine shaft, and surrounding the pool, mountain of rocks waiting for diamond hunters.

"Christopher, we're not looking for diamonds. Crystals, quartz crystals. You'll see. Let me show you how." My father and I climbed a little ways up the rock mountain, and then he asked me to sit. "Now," my father said, "what do you see?"

I looked where he was pointing. I remember his long fingers, his long hands, his smile as he asked again, "What do you see?"

"Rocks."

"Yes, now what about the rocks?"

"Some have different colors?"

"Yes, Christopher. How many different colors?"

"I don't know. Should I count?"

My father didn't want to give me answers, he wanted to point, and point. "There, Chrissy, there. What color?"

"Black."

I picked the black stone and placed it beside my father where he stood.

"And there, Chrissy boy, what?"

"Pink?" I picked up the pink stone and placed it beside the black rock.

And then I started looking a bit to the right and found a rock that looked like gold, and a flat stone with flakes.

Within twenty minutes, as my father stood still and watched, I had collected twenty, thirty different rocks, and I had built a circle of stones around my father as he stood still. And then my father pointed: feldspar, pyrite, mica, granite, and here corundum, and this, coal, and here flecks of gold, real gold, Chrissy, and this, iron, here nickel, and this more feldspar and marble. I looked into the eyes of my father as he smiled. I smiled too. It was in the eyes. He saw something in my eyes. I was in a certain place, a place where he wanted to take me. Real teachers know of this place. It is a place before death, a place to refine disorder.

"Now, you must find a quartz crystal." He sat down beside me and showed me how to pull up rocks, what to look for, where to dig, how to examine a stone for crystals. For half an hour we dug a small hole where we sat until he reached in and pulled out a stone that had a long, clear crystal hanging from its side.

"Diamonds," I whispered.

"Har! Long John Silver would be proud of us," he said.

"Who?" I asked.

"Don't you know *Treasure Island*?"

That afternoon I found three quartz crystals, and I have them still to this day on my desk. Papa. Teacher. To a ten-year-old boy, just a pile of rocks. To an educated man, to a teacher, the rocks are treasures, scientific discoveries, history.

My father still stands there in my memory as he smiles and I see the color of his shoes as he stands in the circle of rocks I found in that year of 1961.

Teachers bring us into the circle of stones. My father brought me into that circle. I wanted to bring my students into that circle when I chose the vocation of teaching, when I stepped into my first classroom in a rural high school in northwestern New Jersey in 1974.

I knew where I wanted to bring my students. I knew that I wanted to point to a certain direction, to a circle of stones, to a certain sound in my voice, to a place that cannot be found without a teacher. The eyes. I wanted to see in the eyes of my students what my father saw in mine when he spoke about crystals.

Where did I want to bring my students? To a place of safety, a secret spot, a land of hope and dreams, down the rabbit hole. I wanted to take my students down the river in a raft. I wanted to take them home in the arms of a father. I wanted to bring them up to the ceiling laughing with Bert and Mary Poppins. I wanted to take my students to the pump and let them feel the water run against their hands as Annie Sullivan screams with joy, "Mrs. Keller! Mrs. Keller! She knows! Helen knows!" I wanted to bring my student's to Anne Frank's attic, and to Claude Brown's America.

There is a place here on earth that contains a field of solace, the furniture of acceptance, the laughter of defeat, the air of comfort, the water of triumph. Such a place has been sought by everyone throughout history.

A true teacher knows of this place and wants to bring his students there each day. A teacher cannot tell his students to follow Alice down the rabbit hole, but he can take their hands and let them feel a deck of cards and ask them to imagine what the Queen of Hearts might look like as she stands in her rose garden. A teacher cannot tell students to feed Helen Keller, but he can ask them to close their eyes and cover their ears and imagine what it is like to be blind and mute. A teacher cannot tell young people to fall in love, but he can ask them to stand on the shore with Gatsby and squint their eyes and try to see the blinking light across the bay.

In my first year as a teacher I asked my class one morning, in preparation for reading a poem by Robert Frost, if they knew any of the constellations.

"Leo," Mr. de Vinck.

"Ursa Major, the bear."

"Mr. de Vinck, Gemini and Pisces."

Aquarius, Cassiopeia, Orion. They knew them all. I was startled. "How do you know these?" I asked. A girl said that they were taught the names of the stars the year before in eighth grade.

"We had to memorize their names. We had a huge test with matching and fill-in-the-blanks. I got a hundred."

"I got them all right except one," a boy said.

"We all got A's on that test. It was part of our final exam," a boy smiled.

"When is the best time to go out and see the stars?" I asked.

No one answered.

"Isn't it fun to look up and point out each constellation?"

No response. The children never went out to look at the stars. I continued with my lesson. "What are the northern lights?"

Silence, but then a boy raised his hand. "Sometimes it's called the aurora borealis."

"Yes, Mark. Do you know anything else?"

"Well, you can see them when you're way up north, or looking out of an airplane. It's like aluminum foil, or looks like that. They are like lights shaking in the sky."

I looked at the boy as he spoke, and I saw, for the first time in my many years as a teacher, a look in his eyes that I saw again and again in twenty years of education. I saw for the first time what my father saw in my eyes: the recognition of that place.

I continued with my lesson. "Does anything exciting ever happen in your lives?" I asked the students.

"My grandmother is coming," a girl volunteered.

"I'm getting a calf to raise for the 4-H Club," another girl said.

"Ah, nothin' happens much around here," a boy suggested.

"Well," I asked the boy, "where can we look for adventure?"

"Television, mostly."

This is when I suddenly just stood before the class. I stopped asking questions, stopped talking. I was suddenly silent. My students looked at me, began to giggle a bit in the uncomfortable silence. Just as they were about to speak, I placed my finger to my lips. "Shhhhh." Then I walked back behind my chair and picked up my briefcase, carried it to the front of the class, and plunked it hard on my desk.

"What are you doing, Mr. de Vinck?"

"Shhhhhhh."

I pretended to be a magician, pulling up my sleeves, pointing in pantomime to my pencil, which I pulled out of my shirt pocket indicating this was my magic wand. I waved the pencil over my briefcase, placed the pencil back into my pocket, then I reach into my bag. I pretended that something grabbed my hand. The children laughed.

"Shhhhhhh." Once again I placed my finger to my lips.

And then I gingerly dipped my hand back into the briefcase, but this time I slowly, slowly pulled out a stack of papers. A boy rolled his eyes. A girl giggled. I gave her a pretend glare of annoyance. "Oh, Mr. de Vinck. You can't even look mean."

"Shhhhhhhh."

I began walking around the classroom, handing each student a sheet of paper from my magic stack. "This is a poem," I began. Groans. "This was written by Robert Frost." More groans. "I am going to read this poem aloud," I whispered, "and then we are going to have a serious test on the poem." Silence.

After I finished handing out the poem to each student, I returned to the front of the class. I waited for the boys and girls to settle down, and then I read aloud:

### On Looking Up By Chance
### At The Constellations

You'll wait a long, long time for anything much
To happen in heaven beyond the floats of cloud
And the Northern Lights that run like tingling
    nerves.
The sun and moon get crossed, but they never
    touch,
Nor strike out fire from each other, nor crash out
    loud.
The planets seem to interfere in their curves,
But nothing ever happens, no harm is done.
We may as well go patiently on with our life,
And look elsewhere than to stars and moon and
    sun

## Friends

For the shocks and changes we need to keep us
    sane.
It is true the longest drought will end in rain,
The longest peace in China will end in strife.
Still it wouldn't reward the watcher to stay awake
In hopes of seeing the calm of heaven break
On his particular time and personal sight.
That calm seems certainly safe to last tonight.

After I read the poem aloud, I stood before the class in silence. I waited and waited and waited, and then I said, "Are you ready for your test?"

"Will it be fill-in-the-blanks?," someone asked?

"Will it count?"

"Can we go over it again?" a girl asked nervously.

"This isn't fair. We didn't have a chance to study," a boy complained.

"Make it a matching test, Mr. de Vinck," a boy said hopefully.

I stood in silence again, and then I just smiled. "Okay, question number one." The students scrambled for their pens and pencils.

"We need paper, Mr. de Vinck."

"Aren't you giving out a test?"

I smiled. "Put your pencils away." I waited. "Question number one: tell me how this poem, in any way, has something to do with you."

Silence. Then someone said, "I've thought about that. How the moon and sun don't bump into each other."

A girl, the one who was looking forward to the arrival of her grandmother, said, "It's true. We have to wait a long time for anything to happen."

We spoke about patience that morning, about the northern lights and China, about the coming rain. They knew about the hope of rain, these farm children. Toward the end of the class, a girl raised her hand. "Mr. de Vinck. What's the second question?"

"Yeah," a boy said, "this is suppose to be a test. How'd we do?"

I returned to my briefcase, pulled out my pen and grade book, and as I read aloud each student's name, I also announced the grade: "Linda: A. Pat: A. Tim, A."

"Are you writing these grades in your book?" a boy asked hopefully.

"Yes."

"But we're all getting A's."

"Yes," I said as I, again, played the magician, returned my pen to my shirt pocket with a flourish, and quietly said, "Shhhhhhhh."

At the end of class, as the students stood up and began leaving the room, I prepared myself for the next set of students, placing another stack of poems in my briefcase. The class was nearly empty when Mark stepped up to my desk. He stood there until all his classmates were gone.

"Mr. de Vinck?"

I looked up from my briefcase. "Yes, Mark?"

"You can see the constellations from the top of my hill at home real clear."

"I bet you can," I answered. "I live forty-five minutes from the George Washington Bridge. Because of the New York lights, I can't see much from my backyard."

"Would you like to see the stars tonight, Mr. de Vinck, from my hill?"

I looked at the boy, and I saw it, in his eyes, that place, that recognition that he saw something in the classroom that I saw. He wasn't consciously aware that he was on his way to Alice's Wonderland, or to Huck Finn's river. I wasn't aware of it either, really. I just felt that, somehow, I had gotten through to this boy in a way that all teachers understand.

"There's no moon tonight," Mark continued. "If you don't want to come, that's all right. You're probably busy." The boy turned and was about to leave the room.

"No, I mean, no I'm not busy, Mark. I'd love to come and see the stars tonight. Is it okay with your parents?"

"Sure."

"How do I get to your house? And what time?"

"The milking is done not so late and the chores and home-work. Could you stop by at 9:30? By that time it's real dark."

"That would be fine," I said.

"I'll draw you a map." The boy folded Frost's poem and tucked it into his back pocket. "Goodbye, Mr. de Vinck."

"Goodbye, Mark. I'll see you later."

After the boy walked out of my room, I looked at the poster I taped to the wall from the poet John Donne:

> Go, and catch a falling star,
> Get with child a mandrake root,
> Tell me, where all past years are,
> Or who cleft the Devil's foot.
> Teach me to hear mermaids singing.

I was free the next period, so I thought I'd buy some juice in the faculty lounge. I stood in the food line behind a history teacher and a guidance counselor. They were trying to decide who the prettiest girl in the senior class was and what chance they would have with her. The history teacher stopped for a moment, turned and said to me, "Chris, when you get to be our ages, you fantasize a lot." Then he and the guidance counselor laughed and each ordered coffee and a Danish. I do not think these men ever heard the mermaids singing.

They invited me to sit with them at the table. This being my first week in school, I thought it was nice of them to extend themselves. I ordered a glass of orange juice and sat with my colleagues. They were talking baseball. Then, out of politeness, the history teacher asked me how my first weeks were going.

"Well, okay I think. A student invited me to his house to see the stars."

"Yeah, can you imagine?," the man said. "I remember when I started teaching, some boys invited me to go bowling. Can you beat that, bowling with a bunch of teenagers? First rule of teaching: don't get involved with the students. I give them my name, rank, and serial number, and the textbook. It's gotten me through twenty years of teaching without a hitch. You'd think they'd know that a teacher has better things do with his life than go bowling." Then he turned to the guidance counselor and said, "Shit, the Giants might take it all this year."

I drank my juice, excused myself, and wondered if John Donne would have gone bowling with a group of fifteen-year-old boys.

When I returned to my class, I found a neatly draw map with a number of red arrows sitting on my desk. At the last arrow Mark had drawn a bright yellow star. A teacher has to dance between the crass and the beautiful.

That afternoon there was a scheduled faculty meeting. The president of the teacher's union distributed the teacher contract and ask that we take a close look and see where adjustments could be made for the following year.

A math teacher complained that the dental plan "stinks." An English teacher said that she was fed up with being assigned to chaperone a dance without compensation. Someone noticed on the school calendar that the Wednesday before the Thanksgiving vacation was listed as a full day. "Ever since I've taught, we've had that as a half-day. Will that still be a half-day? I'll take the whole day as a sick day if I have to."

Following the meeting, John Donne and I graded some papers, then I went to dinner. I wasn't married at the time, so no one was waiting for me. After dinner, I returned to my apartment, watched the news, read a bit, and at 9:00 pulled Mark's map from my briefcase, and stepped outside. A clear night.

I followed the red arrows, my headlights bouncing through the darkness along the rolling Jersey hills. A deer leaped across the road. I turned one corner and found a number of cows sticking their heads through the wood rail fence. I drove on.

On the bottom of Mark's map he had written, "At the Crossings, make a right. About a mile you'll see my house to the left. There are only three houses on this road. Mine is the one with the big picture window. Look for the pumpkin."

I stopped my car for a moment at the entrance to Mark's farm. There, framed in the window of his house, I saw the biggest carved pumpkin I had ever seen. It must have been four feet wide and just as high. A bright light glowed through the pumpkin's triangle eyes and crooked teeth.

At the door I was greeted by Mrs. Miller. Mark stood in the background.

"I hope this is a good time. Mark said it was okay."

"No, no, come in, Mr. de Vinck. This is just fine. Mark told me about your coming. This is fine. Welcome."

"Hi, Mr. de Vinck."

"Hello, Mark. Did you do your homework yet?"

"Yes, sir."

"Mark says that he wants to take you up the hill. I'm sorry about the mud. Would you like to have some coffee and a Danish?"

I smiled. "Yes, yes, thank you very much."

After the coffee and Danish, Mark and I walked into the night. He took me down a small road that lead past a barn. "Watch out for the mud here, Mr. de Vinck."

We stepped around the wet earth, turned to the right and began our climb up the hill. I could smell a distant skunk. The last summer crickets gave out plaintive cries. We walked under some trees, and then we came to a clearing, climbed a few minutes more, then Mark ran ahead, stopped, and called out, "Here, Mr. de Vinck."

As I reached the top of the hill, Mark pointed "Look up, see?" Who was the teacher?

I was so distracted by the mud, the crickets, the skunk, and trees that I had nearly forgotten our mission. I looked up and there a bowl of stars, the entire universe, was lit with clarity and purpose. Mark pointed, "Orion. The Big Dipper. The Twins. Do you see them, Mr. de Vinck?"

"Yes, Mark. And Venus, do you see Venus?"

"That's easy to spot. See the Bear and look," he said with a grand sweep of his arms, "the Milky Way."

"Do you know what the Milky Way is, Mark?"

"Yes, a thick cluster of stars. It looks like a cloud in the sky, doesn't it? But it's a wad of stars."

"Yes, a wad of stars," I laughed.

On that hill, under the stars, Mark told me about his father, who was an airline pilot. "He'd tell us about seeing the northern lights as he flew in from Chicago. He'd see them especially in winter from the left side of his window. I've never seen the northern lights, but my father told me I'd see them someday."

On that hill, under Ursa Major and Gemini and Cassiopeia, Mark Miller told me about his father dying of cancer and how he wanted to be a pilot someday just like his dad. "That's why I liked the poem in class today, Mr. de Vinck, about the northern lights. I brought a flashlight and the poem. I'd like you to read the poem up here."

Mark handed me the flashlight and the folded Robert Frost poem. Under all the universe, as the Great Bear and the Dragon and the Scorpion and a fifteen-year-old boy listened, I read, again, Robert Frost's poem "On Looking Up By Chance At The Constellations."

## Friends

I was a teacher who believed that it was my job to bring my students to understand that wonderful things will happen in their lives. They just have to wait. I was a young teacher hoping to bring my students to the door of peace, so that they could have choices about how they wished to live.

What is this place where teachers want to bring their students? What name? What location? Something about a giant pumpkin framed in a window.

The Robert Frost poem opened a door for Mark, or perhaps it was a door for me. Mark already knew about the stars and laughing bears and dragons that turn over the hills at night when we sleep.

# Antigone, My Friend

∾

One afternoon, between classes, I was walking through the hall and discovered four of my students standing beside a closed locker. They were laughing, acting suspicious. When they saw me, their laughter turned into quiet giggles.

"Hi, you guys. What's up?" I asked.

"Hi, Mr. de Vinck," a girl said. "Nothing."

"We're, ah, watching the world go by," a boy laughed.

"I see." And then I heard a small, muffled laugh. I looked at the students in the hall. They looked at me and smiled, and then I said to the closed locker, "Jan, are you in there?"

The students in the hall roared with laughter as Jan said from somewhere within the wall, "Hi, Mr. de Vinck. I finished my essay for your class."

"Mr. de Vinck," John said. "She's stuck in there. She wanted to see if she could fit in the locker, so she crawled in, then we . . . well, I thought it would be funny if I closed the door. Now she's squeezed in there. I can't turn the locker combination because she's pressing against the door and the lock won't turn."

I tried to spin the combination lock and the door was, indeed, stuck. "Jan, are you all right?"

"Well, it's not too bad in here, Mr. de Vinck. Just a bit dark, though." We all laughed. I stepped into a classroom and called

172

the main office for a custodian. By the time Jan stepped out of the locker, the janitor had cut the lock and unbolted the door from its hinges. There was also a crowd of thirty people waiting for her to step out, including the principal. He suspended her for a day and gave the other four students detention.

On a field trip with 250 students and five buses, we had to pull off the highway and watch Jan run across the wide parking lot to a small gas station. "Hey, I had to go to the bathroom."

On another field trip to an amusement park, ten buses of students had to wait because Jan was missing. It turned out that she went home with some seniors who drove their car down to the park. She was suspended for a week.

Jan smoked in the bathroom. Suspended for three days. Jan swore at a teacher. Detention for three days. She stuffed Limburger cheese in the heating system and caused the evacuation of the entire second floor. Jan was suspended for another week.

When Jan was handed her diploma at graduation, a colleague leaded over and whispered, "I'm glad that *pain* in the ass is gone."

That pain in the ass read the part of Antigone like no other girl in all my years of teaching.

That pain in the ass once dressed up like Emily Dickinson, lit a candle, and read aloud from the "Belle at Amherst."

Jan wrote a paper about crossing a wood bridge with her little sister. I will never forget a line she wrote, "Over the water, we stopped, and Kara threw a leaf into the stream and said, 'Look, Jan, there I go.'"

Jan took private dancing lessons, sent me a sympathy card when my grandmother died, dated many boys (and didn't make love to one of them, she proudly told me once). She hung pictures of movie stars and Gandhi in her locker. Her father was an alcoholic, her mother a strong woman. At her graduation, she waved and waved her diploma over her head. I should have leaned over to my colleague and I should have said, "Not a pain in the ass, sir, but Antigone." Instead, I just felt ashamed.

Sophocles wrote, "Numberless are the world's wonders, but none more wonderful than man." How many teachers saw how wonderful Jan was? How many teachers deeply understand that each child who comes into their classroom is truly wonderful?

I have seen teachers humiliate children, parents scream at children, administrators embarrass children. We've seen on national television administrators raising baseball bats to children. We send children to school buildings that are falling apart, that don't have heat, materials, books. We dump standardized tests on children, we classify them, track them, grade them, shuffle them from class to class. We give them numbers, lockers, homework, schedules. We try to force a book of virtues down their throats, force school prayer upon them, brand national standards onto their skin, make them pledge the flag, bounce them around in school buses, but do we love the children? Do we see their uniqueness? Do we celebrate their differences, their abilities, their smiles and tears? Do we recognize their wonder?

A child who is loved is a child who will understand prayer. A child who is loved will pledge to the flag, pledge to his teachers, pledge to his friends and family an allegiance to a whole community that celebrates his existence. Mr. Rogers says to the children of America on a daily basis, "I like you just the way you are." He tells the children that "it is such a good feeling to know that you're alive."

Schools today are trying to fix what a child is not, when we ought to be building up on what a child is.

Do the teachers in our nation tremble before the glory of the children who walk into their classrooms each morning?

# Friends

Many years later I received a letter sent to my home. It was from Jan. This is, in part, what she said:

> When I left high school I didn't know what I wanted to do with my life. I struggled through college. My father died. My mother never remarried. Remember in the play, just after the King condemned Antigone to death, the chorus sings this lament:
>
> > Love, unconquerable
> > Waster of rich men, keeper
> > Of warm lights and all-night vigil
> > In the soft face of a girl:
> > Sea-wanderer, forest-visitor!
> > Even the pure immortals cannot escape you,
> > And mortal man, in his one day's dusk,
> > Trembles before your glory.
>
> You don't know, but I wrote down those lines in my journal after your class that day because I felt that you saw the soft face of me, that you cared about me, that maybe you even loved me in a way that my father couldn't. I just wanted to tell you this. I am doing fine. I am married. My husband works for the phone company. We have three children, girls, and each day I tremble in their glory. You helped me see this in my children. You helped me see this in myself.

~ *Conclusion* ~

In this morning's newspaper the business section is full of optimism: "Wall Street Bonuses Were Big," "A Banking Dynasty on the Move," "Consumer Confidence and Home Sales Surge," "Underwriting Roars Back in Quarter," "Deal Creates International Hotel Empire," "British Pound at Four-Year High."

Each day the paper devotes on average eleven pages listing stock-market indicators from the New York Stock Exchange, American Stock Exchange, Nasdaq, Dow Jones, Standard and Poor's, foreign stocks, futures markets, and mutual funds.

We, as a nation of business, pay close attention to the value of our investments, to the profits we earn, and to the dividends we transfer into our accounts. We take risks, calculate profit margins, generate excitement, speculate, buy, sell, acquire, merge. From our labors we glean a standard of success: wealth.

America is built on success, and by all accounts, we are a successful nation, yet why is there a painted smile on the face of America? How do we feel when we drive home each day, or when we are lying in bed at night contemplating the day's events or the next day's strategy?

The old saying, Be careful what you wish for because you might get it, is appropriate here. Ask most young people what they wish for these days, and they will tell you: fame and money.

Ask the man or woman sitting in the back seat of a stretch limo what it is he or she is pursuing this morning, and the answer will be cryptic but will mean the same thing: "fame and money." And each day we have a running list of winners and losers on the stock market page, yet how many of us whisper at night, "Though the hand of my wealth tickles me, my heart aches."

When I was a teacher I often told my students that there was nothing wrong with wishing for fame and money. Everyone loves attention and mahogany, but I also often said to the teenagers that if a satisfied ego and comfort were their ultimate goals in life, they would eventually be buried in silk robes and in anonymous graves.

What, then, can bring a smile of truth to the face of Arthur Miller's Willie Loman? Remember, all he really wanted was attention, after all, the same thing we all crave. He wanted to love and to be loved, but as hard as I tried, as much as I scanned the financial section today, squinted at the fine print and various numbers, I could not find anything that measured the nation's sense of success by our ability to love and to be loved.

We place in the center of our American attention the wrong goals. Nice guys should finish *first*. But men and women in our country are judged on their bank accounts, physical appearance, cars, power, and prestige, not on their ability to be nice.

We took Thomas Jefferson's eyeglasses and focused them on laying down railroad tracks and asphalt, building glass towers and rocket ships.

Steam poured through our generators, oil and the atom ignited an explosion into the twentieth century. Television gave extraordinary attention to steel, plastic, false drama, and the laugh track.

We rock the ages with the sweat of our work, and with the pull and tug of ourselves as we lurch toward the cities in the new cycle of extinction: the commute. We labor to polish the image, create advantages for ourselves, and speed up the carousel so that we can make more frequent grabs at the gold ring. We reward ourselves with comfort, and check in with the daily report card: the stock pages. But how do we feel at the end of the day?

We are pushed to believe that money and fame are at the center of success in our lives. We have been given a vision of paradise, a place of success to be attained, and we buy into it each day. John Kenneth Galbraith wrote a wonderful line in his book *The New Industrial State*: "We are becoming the servants in thought, as in action, of the machine we have created to serve us."

We think like machines, we act like machines, we dream like machines, we are fed like machines, and we fight our own obsolescence with new oils and polish. We are becoming the servants of the machine and forgetting the hippopotamuses.

You will not find on any stock page an account of hippo-potamuses sloshing peacefully in a mud hole at the edge of a summer veldt. We are not taught, any longer, to see with a unique vision ourselves and the world.

Do we risk thinking at night, before we go to sleep, about the nature of a child dying from cancer, or risk investing in a memory of Christmas? Do we profit from a son calling us for help, or calculate the dividends of God? What is the profit margin of saying thank you or inviting a neighbor over for dinner? What if we speculate on the value of faith, hope, and charity, or ask a broker to wage a deal on the day's current price on gratitude?

Do not get me wrong. Wealth, beauty, comfort are wonder-ful byproducts of our system of business, but I believe this system is being given uneven attention to the loss of the system of living that we established for ourselves a little over two hundred years ago.

We had a system of beliefs built into our historical docu-ments, a vision of life based on liberty, justice, God, family, freedom, art, humor, patience, compassion, victory, stamina, children, courage. But these things are not gauged each day by our newspapers. These things are not celebrated. These things are not held out to us each day as a reward for our wise investments and risk taking.

We fool ourselves into gasping at the next beautiful car off the assembly line, or the newest rock star, or the next surge in the stock market. We do not gasp any longer when a man and woman exchange wedding vows, or when a child learns how to read.

We have created a machine that wants us to be delighted, and at the end of such delight wants us to spend our money on the occasion of such amazement. But the delight is artificially created, bought with hope and anticipation, and at night, in bed, we feel, somehow empty.

*How* we live and *why* we live are not being given equal attention in our country today. How we are to dress, work, learn, eat, play are being defined, refined, explained to us each day with billions of dollars invested in marketing, research, sales, and production. But *why* we are living from day to day is examined, by obligation, in our churches once a week, defined by poets who are unread, and by children of hope who set out on summer afternoons with an older brother looking for salamanders.

We do not consult a broker for the best deal in compassion, do not have a stock indicator of our loneliness. We are forgetting how to see what is most valuable to ourselves, to our children, and to our neighbors. We are giving too much attention to the *business* of living and too little attention to the "stock portfolio" of our personal lives.

Do we want our children to grow up with financial tunnel vision or the vision of a saint? Albert Schweitzer wrote in his autobiography *Out of My Life and Thought*, "Late on the third day, at the very moment when, at sunset, we were making our way through a herd of hippopotamuses, there flashed upon my mind, unforeseen and unsought, the phrase, 'Reverence for Life.'"

We are being cut off from the hippopotamuses, from the awe, from the vision of delight about what we see, who we are and what we love. William Ellery Channing wrote in 1843, "The mind, in proportion as it is cut off from free communication with nature, with revelation, with God, with itself, loses its life, just as the body droops when debarred from the air and the cheering light from heaven."

There exist dividends from another system: love's harvest. They can be earned from family, faith, and friends. These are some of the stock dividends that can, if we take the risk of seeing again as we did as children, come from the cheering light of heaven.

The dividends of our own success can be calculated in our beds at night just before we sleep as we listen for either the distant clang of gold coins or for the laughter of love as we swim side by side with the hippopotamuses.

## Also by Christopher de Vinck

*The Power of the Powerless*
*Augusta and Trab*
*Only the Heart Knows How to Find Them*
*Songs of Innocence and Experience*
*Simple Wonders*
*Thread of Paradise*
*The Book of Moonlight*

# OF RELATED INTEREST

Teresa Rhodes McGee
## THE COMFORTER
*Stories of Loss and Rebirth*
Ten vivid stories written from the heart of a gifted
storyteller—true stories about unforgettable people who
find a tenacity for life, often amidst an ocean of pain.
*0-8245-1567-6; $14.95*

Paula D'Arcy
## GIFT OF THE RED BIRD
The heart's deep yearning for God, and God's answer, are
vividly described in the story of Paula D'Arcy's vision
quest, a three-day wilderness experience that follows years
of grief recovery after the terrible deaths of her husband
and baby.
*0-8245-1590-0; $14.95*

*At your bookstore or, to order directly from the publisher, please
send check of money order (including $3.00 shipping for the first
book and $1.00 for each additional book) to:*

THE CROSSROAD PUBLISHING COMPANY
370 LEXINGTON AVENUE, NEW YORK, NY 10017

*We hope you enjoyed* Love's Harvest. *Thank you
for reading it.*

crossroad